The Word

The Word

A GUIDE TO UNDERSTANDING
AND ENJOYING THE BIBLE

Dr. Bob Beltz

ISBN: 1517465176
ISBN 13: 9781517465179
Library of Congress Control Number: 2015915670
CreateSpace Independent Publishing Platform
North Charleston, South Carolina

In Memory of
Dr. Vernon Grounds friend, mentor, hero.

Preface

§

A NUMBER OF YEARS AGO I wrote a book titled, *Becoming a Man of the Word*. At the time, I had been writing a series of books used in men's ministry across the country. I found myself repeatedly giving women "permission" to read the book. The content was not exclusively masculine by any means, but the publisher wanted to target men.

That book went out of print this year. Rather than simply republishing it for men, I decided to make a few adjustments and give the book the co-ed audience it always deserved. What you have in your hands (or on your Kindle or iPad) is that book.

Contents

Introduction

§

I LOVE THE BIBLE. THERE is no book in the world like it. I believe it is accurately called the Word of God, and that when I sit down and read it, the living God communicates with me.

I did not always feel this way. As a twenty-year-old university student, I was an agnostic. I openly professed that I thought the Bible was simply the creation of men. I thought it contained myth and historical error, and in discussions concerning religion I would say so. Of course, I had never actually read it. I was simply parroting ideas some professor had spoken. When I am confronted with the same arguments today, my first question is always, "Have you ever *read* the Bible?" Nearly every time the response is, "No"!

This is a book about the Bible. More accurately, this is a book about a man or woman's relationship with the Bible. I aspire to be a man of the Word. I don't consider myself as having attained the spiritual maturity to call myself that. But I'd like to be. I hope that someday, when I'm remembered by friends and family, they might say, "He loved the Bible!" It is my hope in writing this book that someday that same epitaph might apply to you.

Bob Beltz
Littleton, Colorado September 9, 2015

CHAPTER 1

Old Testament History

§

Oh give me that book! At any price, give me the book of God!

— John Wesley

It was a beautiful spring evening when my friend Rich Beach called me into his room. He had a huge grin on his face as he handed me a package wrapped in gift paper. I opened it, and inside was a Bible. I had been a believer in Jesus Christ for about six months and had developed the discipline of reading the Bible every day.

But this Bible was different from my Bible. This one had both the Old Testament and the New Testament in it. For six months I had been reading only the New Testament. Having grown up in a home where the Bible was not read and where church attendance was sporadic at best, it hadn't even dawned on me that I might want to read the *whole* book!

Up until that night, mastery of the Bible seemed like an achievable task. Now, the information required to be theologically savvy had nearly tripled! Suddenly, I realized once again that I was truly biblically challenged.

WELCOME TO THE BIBLE

"The Bible" is the name we give the world's most unique book. The title is simply the translation of the Greek word *biblos*, which means "book." The Bible is The Book! Spanning the ages, from the beginning of time as we know it to a future we can barely comprehend, beyond time and space, it tells the story of God's love for us and the implications of that love for life on this planet we call Earth. The book recounts how life was intended to be, what went wrong, and what God has done, is doing, and will do to make things right. To borrow the title of the classic film, it is "the greatest story ever told."

ROUTE 66

As we study the Bible, it is important to recognize that the one book we call the Bible is actually a collection of sixty-six separate documents. Often these individual documents are them- selves referred to as "books." For instance, you might hear someone talk about the book of Ephesians. What has been labeled "Ephesians" in our New Testament is actually a letter written by the apostle Paul to the group of men and women that comprised the church in the city of Ephesus. It is not a book in our traditional way of understanding the idea of book.

Most of the original documents that make up our modern Bible were written on scrolls. There was no one book that you could go to a bookstore and purchase. Actually, there were no bookstores or printing presses when the contents of these various scrolls began to be placed together in a single volume. These collections were copied by hand and considered to be great treasures. The Jewish men who copied these documents were called scribes. Later, after the New Testament came into existence, monks — also taking the title of scribe — hand-copied these volumes. There were special rooms called *scriptoria* in many monasteries where men spent their entire lives making copies of the Bible.

THE TWO DIVISIONS

The Bible has two main divisions — the break between those books written before the time of Christ and those containing the history of Jesus and the early church. These divisions are labeled "the Old Testament" and "the New Testament."

The word *testament* could also be understood as *covenant*. A covenant is an agreement or contract made between two parties. In this case, the parties are God and humanity. The concepts of old and new date back to the sixth century before Jesus, when the prophet Jeremiah spoke of a time when God was going to enter into a new "contract" with the nation of Israel (Jeremiah 31:31). When Jesus met with his disciples in the Upper Room in Jerusalem the night before he was crucified, he told them his death on the cross would institute this new covenant of which Jeremiah spoke (Matthew 26:28).

Thirty-nine of the Bible's documents fall into the category of the Old Testament, twenty-seven into the New. Add the two together and you get sixty-six. I often think of the Bible as a spiritual adventure down God's Route 66.

When the Bible was first being gathered together — a process called canonization — these sixty-six documents were often arranged according to the type of literature they contained. In most of our Bibles we have seven distinct groupings (which we will follow in this book). The first of these consists of seventeen books that contain the history of the nation of Israel from the time of its origins, around 2000 B.C., until the end of the Old Testament era, about 400 B.C. This latter date ended the period of restoration and rebuilding after the Babylonian Captivity of the sixth century B.C. Our objective in the rest of this chapter will be to understand the history contained in these seventeen books.

Understanding Old Testament History

Genesis

The first book of the Bible is titled "Genesis" in our English bibles. In the original Hebrew text it was titled "In the beginning," the opening phrase of the document. Genesis is a book of origins. It tells the stories of the origin of the universe, the origin of humanity, the origin of evil, and the origin of the nation Israel. If you do not understand Genesis, you will never understand the rest of the Bible.

Genesis can be divided into two major parts. The first part (chapters 1–11) is composed of four major events of primeval history. The second part (chapters 12–50) tells the stories of four major characters: the Patriarchs.

Primeval History. The first event highlighted in Genesis is the creation of the universe. The message is clear: God is the Creator, (1:1). God spoke and the universe came into existence. From primordial chaos he fashions the cosmos into an ordered place occupied by plants, animals, and ultimately, a being created in his own image — Man. Although Genesis was never intended to be a science book, there is adequate evidence to support the scientific integrity of the simple picture of Creation depicted in Genesis 1–2. From a literary standpoint, it is obvious the primary message is that God is the Creator of a purposeful universe in which humanity plays a central role.

The word picture given us here is of a utopian environment in which God lives in loving relationship with all he has made. All is good, (1:4,10,12,18,21,25,31). In fact, God provides man with everything needed to live a blessed and fulfilled life — right down to a life partner called woman.

After painting this idyllic portrait of life as it was meant to be, the logical question to ask is, "What went wrong?" The second major event of Genesis answers this question. Theologians refer to this incident as the Fall. It explains the origins of virtually every problem that besets the human race to this day.

To be created in the image of God involves the capacity for choice. Relationship requires decisions. God did not create robots. He gave the people he created moral freedom. The downside of such a reality was the ability humanity possessed to reject God's role as God and to act autonomously, in opposition to him. This is exactly what transpires in Genesis 3. The results have shaped the course of human history and provide the logical foundation for all that follows in the Bible.

John Milton speaks of this in his most famous work, *Paradise Lost*. The message of the Bible's love story is that the lover was rejected. Utopia was lost. Death and distortion entered the created order, disfiguring not only humanity's relationship with God, but also humanity's relationship with nature. Interpersonal relationships and even man's internal psychic landscape became distorted from their original divine design. The Bible refers to these fallen realities by using the term *cursed* (3:17).

The consequences of the Fall are played out in the next two events in the book of Genesis — the Flood, and the scattering of nations and the confusion of languages at the Tower of Babel.

By the end of the first eleven chapters of Genesis, we see a world much like the one we live in today — a world distorted from the original intentions of the Creator, a world in need of divine intervention.

Fortunately, this is the beginning of the story, not the end. The bulk of the Bible is concerned with what God has done and is going to do to restore that which was lost, hence the title of Milton's subsequent classic, *Paradise Regained.*

The Patriarchs. There is a sense in which the first eleven chapters of Genesis are primarily designed to introduce the events that open chapter 12. It is here that we are introduced to a Chaldean urbanite named Abram, the first link in a chain of men and women who will launch a plan to bring humanity back into proper relationship with God. Genesis 12 is the interpretive key to the rest of the Bible.

God appeared to a man named Abram while he was living in the ancient city of Ur on what is today called the Persian Gulf. The encounter, initiated by God, involved a challenge and a series of promises. Here we see the concept of a covenant at work. God offered to enter into a contract with Abram.

God instructed Abram to leave his home and his father's family and to head for a place that God would show him. If Abram would go, God would "bless" him (12:3). The biblical concept of blessing is the opposite of the concept of the curse. It involves the consequences or outcomes of getting back into the proper relationship with God, a theme that runs throughout the rest of the Bible.

If Abram would follow God's instructions, God promised that his descendants would become a great nation and a source of blessing to all the nations of the earth (12:3). Ultimately, this promise would lead to the coming of Jesus and all he did to restore us to a love relationship with God.

So Abram left the comfort of the city of Ur and headed toward the land of Canaan where his descendants would eventually become the nation we call Israel. In the process he was given a new name, Abraham, meaning "father of multitudes." The rest of the book of Genesis is the story of four generations of this family. Abraham had two sons — Ishmael, through his wife's servant Hagar, and Isaac, the son of a supernatural pregnancy in his wife Sara's old age. God made it clear that his promises would be fulfilled through the line of Isaac (17:19).

Like Abraham, Isaac also had two sons, Esau and Jacob. Although Jacob was the one through whom God's promises would find ongoing fulfillment, the story of the two brothers is one of deception and manipulation. After deceiving his father and provoking the anger of his brother, Jacob was forced to flee for his life and ended up halfway back to Ur in the city of Haran. There he married and eventually had twelve sons. After twenty-two years away from Canaan, Jacob finally headed home. On the way he had a life-changing encounter with God (32:24-30). His twelve sons would eventually become the heads of twelve clans, or tribes that would one day become a nation in fulfillment of the promise made to Abraham. The nation would bear Jacob's new name — Israel.

The final chapters of Genesis focus on Joseph, one of the twelve sons. Sold into slavery by his brothers, Joseph ascended to a place of prominence in Egypt second only to Pharaoh. God used Joseph to save the lives of his brothers and to position this nomadic family to become the great nation he promised Abraham it would become.

Exodus and Leviticus

Genesis forms the foundation for understanding all that follows in the historical books of the Old Testament. By the end of the book, all seventy of Abraham's descendants are living in Egypt where they have gone to survive a worldwide famine. There in Egypt, over a period of four hundred years, the seventy grow to a people group of approximately three million. This is where the story picks up in Exodus.

Exodus is the second book in what is often called the Pentateuch, the first five books of the Old Testament. These books were sometimes called the Torah, or Law. That title was also used at times to refer to the entire body of historical books.

The exodus of the children of Israel out of Egypt and back to the land of Canaan involved the intervention of God in such a dramatic way that the events have stood at the heart of Jewish culture and religion for nearly 3,400 years. Exodus begins with the story of Moses. He was the man God called to lead the nation out of what had become a living hell. He was one of the greatest leaders of recorded history and the central figure in Israel's early history.

The Pharaoh refused Moses' God-given demand to let the Israelites leave Egypt. Obviously, he was reluctant to lose his free labor source! So God used Moses and his brother Aaron to inflict a series of catastrophes on the Egyptians to motivate Pharaoh to change his mind. The final of ten catastrophes, or plagues, involved the death of the firstborn male of every family in the land. But with this judgment, God also provided a way of deliverance. If a family would kill a lamb and place its blood around the doorways of their house, God promised that when the Angel of Death moved over the land, he would "pass over" every house so protected (12:13).

This final plague led to the release and freedom of the people of Israel. The Exodus account tells how this mass of humanity left Egypt and traveled to Mount Sinai. Here God again expressed his love by giving the Israelites a set of life instructions to help restore their relationship with him. We call these instructions the Law, and they included the basis of modern civilized society — the Ten Commandments (20:1-17).

Along with these instructions, God also designed a system to deal with failure to perfectly follow them. This system centered on a tent called the tabernacle. It was here that the nation could bring substitute sacrifices to temporarily atone for their shortcomings. It was also at this tent where God would tangibly manifest his presence above a gold-covered box called the Ark of the Covenant in an fifteen-by-fifteen foot room called the Holy of Holies. Details concerning the tabernacle and the sacrifices that were offered there are contained in the book of Leviticus.

It was also during these encounters on Mount Sinai that God revealed his name. In the ancient world, the concept of knowing a god's name indicated a relationship of intimacy. When Moses asked God for this information, God revealed that his name is YHWH. These four letters in Hebrew are variously translated as "I AM," "I cause to be," and "I will be who I will be" (3:14). From this point forward, it was YHWH who Israel worshiped and served.

NUMBERS

After the encampment at Mount Sinai, Moses led the people to the borders of the Promised Land of Canaan. This section of history is contained in the fourth book of the Old Testament: Numbers.

The record of the Bible, and extraneous historical documents, reveal that the Canaanite culture had become morally and spiritually bankrupt. From God's perspective, the nations occupying Canaan had reached a point beyond salvage. God would judge these nations by sending Israel to defeat them and dispossess them of the land he had promised to Abraham.

Upon reaching the borders of the Promised Land, Moses sent a group of twelve spies into southern Canaan. Ten of these spies returned with an extremely pessimistic report that discouraged the people of Israel. Instead of obeying God's instructions to move forward the people refused to enter the land. As a result, for forty years the Israelites wandered in the wilderness of the Sinai Peninsula until every fighting man twenty years of age and older had died. Only two men of this generation, Joshua and Caleb, entered the land after these forty years, but I'll let you read the book to find out why.

The book of Numbers ends with a census of the nation. The name of the book, Numbers or Numbering, comes from the fact that a census was taken at the beginning of the book and again at the end. By the closing chapters of Numbers, the nation sits encamped on the east bank of the Jordan River, opposite the city of Jericho.

DEUTERONOMY

The opening of Deuteronomy, the fifth and final book of the Pentateuch, occurs roughly forty years after the events at Mount Sinai. As the nation prepared to enter and possess the land, Moses reminded a new generation of the hard lesson their parents had learned and gave the Law a second time. (Appropriately enough, Deuteronomy is a word from the Greek translation of the Old Testament that means, "Second Law.") The three speeches contained in this book contain the final words of Moses before he handed the nation's leader- ship reins to Joshua.

JOSHUA

The actual conquest and occupation of what was known as the Promised Land took place sometime between 1450 and 1250 A.D. Biblical scholars hotly debate the specific dates of the conquest, often on the basis of archeological evidence that, ironically, confirms the actual events. Leadership of the nation had already been transferred from Moses to Joshua. The history of this next period is contained in the book that bears his name.

Joshua is the first of twelve books that follow the Pentateuch and contain the remainder of the historical data concerning ancient Israel. Joshua successfully led the nation across the Jordan and into the land. Strategic victories at Jericho and Ai effectively cut the land in two. Two military campaigns, one against the northern Canaanite peoples and one against those groups living in the south, were immensely successful. By the end of these campaigns only small pockets of resistance remained.

Unfortunately, these pockets would cause the Israelites untold difficulties for centuries to come.

The twelve tribes (now actually thirteen since the tribe of Joseph had been divided into the two "half-tribes" of Ephraim and Manasseh, Joseph's two sons born in Egypt) settled down to occupy the land God had promised them and to fulfill the destiny God had designed.

The books of Exodus through Joshua cover less than one hundred years of Israel's history, yet they were extremely important years that shaped the future of the nation. Once we move into the book of Judges, the pace picks up dramatically. In this one small book we will move through four hundred years of history by means of a series of short narratives. These narratives revolve around the lives of a handful of charismatic leaders we call judges.

JUDGES AND RUTH

The book of Judges covers Israel's history from the time the nation occupied Canaan to the beginning of the monarchy. This four-hundred-year period is marked by a series of seven cycles. This was a time when what we think of as the nation Israel was actually composed of thirteen independent clans loosely held together by their common heritage and religious belief system.

The picture painted here might be thought of as a rationale for the nation moving toward a monarchy form of government. Certainly, it's not a bright period in Israel's history. It was marked by repeated divergence from following God's law, resulting in spiritual and moral rebellion. God responded to Israel's rebellion by allowing foreign invaders to conquer the nation. The hope of the nation rested with those people God raised up to restore the nation to faithfulness. These men (and one woman) were called *shaphat* in the Hebrew text. We translate this word as *judge* in most of our English translations, but it actually means "a restorer of righteousness."

There are seven primary cycles in the book and seven major judges. Some of the more colorful characters in biblical history appear during this period, including Gideon, Deborah, and Samson.

The message of Judges is summarized in its final verse: "In those days Israel had no king; everyone did as he saw fit" (21:25). In the midst of this time of spiritual decay, the book of Ruth tells the story of one woman whom God honored for her faithfulness. The relationship he orchestrated between Ruth and a man named Boaz produced a son who became part of the lineage of Jesus.

1–2 SAMUEL

The final verse of Judges serves as a perfect introduction to the next historical book. In our English Bibles this book is called 1 Samuel and is followed by its sequel, 2 Samuel. In the Hebrew versions of the Old Testament these two books were combined and simply called Samuel. The later division was probably the result of the book's contents being written on two scrolls.

First Samuel introduces the last of the judges, the first of the classical prophets, and the first king of a united Israel. The transitional figure is a man named Samuel, who is both the last judge of the tribal confederacy and the first prophet of the monarchy.

The period of Israel's monarchy can be divided into two distinct stages. The first is the period of the United Kingdom, which lasted only 120 years. The three kings of this era — Saul, David, and Solomon — are probably the best known of Israel's history. Each reigned over a united nation of thirteen tribes for a period of forty years.

First Samuel specifically records the reign of King Saul, the first monarch of a nation that was never intended to have an earthly king. The anointing and coronation of Saul marked the end of Israel's life as a theocracy. In other words, God was rejected as king because Israel demanded an earthly king. The story of Saul is a tragic one.

Anointed by the prophet Samuel, Saul was further anointed by the Spirit of God, who empowered him to fulfill the role for which he had been called. At first it looked like Saul was a great choice. He immediately defeated Israel's enemies and united this diverse group of tribal clans. Unfortunately, the rest of 1 Samuel is a record of Saul's decline into disaster. The final chapter of the book finds the army of Israel defeated by the Philistine army, with Saul's sons lying dead at his feet as he falls on his own sword and kills himself (31:1-4).

In the midst of Saul's reign, God picked his replacement: a man God identified as "a man after my own heart." His name was David. The book of 1 Samuel includes many of David's greatest exploits, including the famous battle with the giant Goliath (17:1-50). However, it is not until 2 Samuel that David's reign as king is recorded.

One of the unique qualities of biblical history is how honestly the Bible tells the whole story. Most ancient histories tended to highlight, and even exaggerate, the positive acts of its kings. The Bible is brutally honest about the flaws of its heroes. The record of David's life is one such example.

David is considered by many to be the greatest king of Israel. It was during his reign that Israel reached its Golden Age. He finally defeated the Philistine threat that had harassed the nation for decades. He moved the tabernacle to the newly captured city of Jerusalem and centralized both worship and government. For forty years David was the model monarch — almost. At the height of success David committed adultery with the wife of one his military leaders and orchestrated his murder. The incident with Bathsheba was a dark page in David's personal history. Although he repented and was forgiven, the consequences of his action colored the remaining years of his rule.

KINGS AND CHRONICLES

If you are reading through the biblical history of Israel expecting a clear sense of chronology, it is at this point that things get a bit confusing. The combined books of Samuel and Kings give a chronological record of this period of time. After the book of 2 Kings you will find two more historical books, 1–2 Chronicles.

The books of Chronicles cover much of the same time period as Samuel and Kings, but from a slightly different angle. First Chronicles covers the reign of David, but without any of the negative events recorded in 2 Samuel. Second Chronicles covers the same period of history as 1–2 Kings, but from the perspective of the Southern kingdom of Judah. I will explain in a moment the division of the kingdom into two separate kingdoms, but for now I want you to understand how these books fit together.

1 KINGS (2 CHRONICLES)

At the height of its glory, David turned the throne of Israel over to his son Solomon. Solomon is one of the more colorful characters in the Old Testament. Although he was known for his gift of wisdom, Solomon's reign was definitely a mixed bag. The nation enjoyed forty years of peace from external threats during his rule. Solomon built the temple that his father only dreamed of building. He engaged in massive building projects, and the personal wealth he amassed was legendary.

Near the end of his reign, opposition began to develop from within the kingdom. His personal wealth and the glory of building the nation came at a heavy toll, especially for the northern tribes, who were feeling the burden of stiff taxation.

Upon Solomon's death, the throne of Israel passed to his son Rehoboam. For many of us, the names of the kings and the history of Israel begin to become a bit more obscure at this point. Rehoboam was not a wise man. Heeding the advice of his younger cronies instead of the wisdom of Israel's elders, Rehoboam pushed the nation into full-blown civil war. The ten northern tribes defected and the period of the United Kingdom came to an end.

2 KINGS (2 CHRONICLES)

The history of the Divided Kingdom actually begins with 1 Kings 12, and runs through the end of 2 Kings. Again, remember that these two books were originally one, being arbitrarily divided on the basis of scroll length. This same period of history is contained in 2 Chronicles.

The leader of the tribe of Ephraim, a man named Jeroboam, led these northern tribes in rebellion against Solomon's son Rehoboam around 930 B.C. From that time until the end of the Old Testament period, the nation we think of as Israel was actually composed of two nations. The Northern Kingdom, initially ruled by Jeroboam, maintained the name Israel. The Southern Kingdom, consisting of the tribes of Judah and Benjamin, became known as Judah.

From the time of the nation's division until the demise of the Northern Kingdom, nineteen kings ruled the North over a two-hundred-year span. The book of 2 Kings lists every king of the North and gives the exact assessment of every king's reign. The phrase that occurs repeatedly is, "He did evil in the eyes of the Lord."

When Jeroboam created the northern alliance, he realized he had a problem. The unifying force of the nation had been its relationship to YHWH. But the focus of YHWH worship was centered on the Temple in Jerusalem, smack dab in the middle of the Southern kingdom. Jeroboam responded to this dilemma by creating a competing religious system with its own temple and priesthood. He led the ten tribes of the North into idolatry. Every king that followed him did the same.

For two hundred years, God sent messengers called prophets to warn the northern tribes to return to him or face judgment. We will see in chapter 3 how the books of prophecy relate to the historical books. For now, understand that not one northern king listened to the prophets God sent. As a consequence, in 722 B.C., God used the nation of Assyria to wage war against the Northern kingdom and defeat it.

One of the more confusing dimensions of 2 Kings is how it moves back and forth between Israel and Judah when listing kings. The listing is actually chronological, not geographical. As long as one king remained in power in either North or South, the next king listed is the king of the other kingdom.

For example, Jeroboam reigned for twenty-two years, while Rehoboam only reigned for seventeen. Three more kings reigned over Judah while Jeroboam was still on the northern throne. These three are listed before another king of the North is listed. Abijah came to the southern throne in the eighteenth year of Jeroboam's reign. Two years later Asa, who took the throne of Judah in the twentieth year of Jeroboam's reign, followed him. Asa reigned for the next forty-one years in Judah, so an entire string of northern kings are listed before another king of Judah appears in the book. You get the hang of it.

Second Chronicles is not nearly as confusing when you realize it only contains the records of the kings of Judah. The Southern Kingdom had a longer history than the North. The reason for this is very simple. The Southern Kingdom of Judah had twenty kings (one queen). Of these rulers, you will find occurrences in the text where the assessment of the king reads, "He did what was right in the eyes of the Lord."

The reforms instituted by these good kings gave the Southern Kingdom a life span almost 150 years longer than the North. In the same way that God sent messengers to the kings of the North, he sent them to the kings of the South. The difference between the southern and northern kings was that these good kings listened to what God said through his prophets.

Eventually, however, Judah also reached a point of spiritual deterioration that led to God's judgment. This time the agent of judgment was the kingdom of Babylon. In three separate campaigns the Babylonians defeated the Southern Kingdom. The final campaign came in 586 B.C. when the city of Jerusalem and the Temple were destroyed and the surviving citizens were carried into captivity. Both 2 Kings and 2 Chronicles end with accounts of the fall of Jerusalem. Second Chronicles adds an introduction to the final period of Israel's history — the period of the restoration from captivity.

EZRA, NEHEMIAH, AND ESTHER

The final three historical books tell of the return from captivity and give a glimpse into some of the events in the land of captivity that set the stage for Israel's return. Ezra and Nehemiah record the Southern Kingdom's return from captivity and the rebuilding of Jerusalem. The events highlight three main characters and involve three rebuilding projects. Although the title of the first book is Ezra, it might as well have been Zerubbabel. He is the first of the three main characters.

In 539 B.C., seventy years after the first of the deportations from Jerusalem, the Medo-Persian Empire under Cyrus defeated the Babylonian Empire. As prophesied by Jeremiah and Isaiah, Cyrus issued a decree that a remnant of the Jewish people should return to Jerusalem and rebuild the temple. This remnant was led by Zerubbabel and headed back to Jerusalem in 538 B.C.

Construction had barely begun on the Temple when opposition arose from the inhabitants of the land who stood to lose their power should the Jews succeed. Their opposition effectively brought the work to a stop until the time of Darius, the next Medo-Persian king. The story of how the work was motivated to begin again is found in chapter 3 in this book, where we look at the messages of the prophets of this restoration period.

The second main character of the restoration period was Ezra, a priest skilled in teaching God's Word. During the reign of the Persian king Xerxes, Ezra was commissioned to return to Israel to encourage the rebuilding process, especially the people's spiritual condition. His ministry was the unifying factor that ties the books of Ezra and Nehemiah together. In the Hebrew Bible these books formed one document named Esras, and later the two were known as 1–2 Ezra.

The third primary figure of this period was a man named Nehemiah, who served as the cupbearer to King Artaxerxes. In 445 B.C. Artaxerxes issued the decree to rebuild the walls of Jerusalem. Without walls, the city continued to lie desolate. (In these times, a city was not a city until it had walls.) And though Nehemiah also encountered resistance, because of his strong leadership the walls were completed and dedicated in a miraculous fifty-two days. Jerusalem sat ready to reclaim its destiny.

While the drama of these events filled the stage of the Holy Land, the drama in the land of captivity was just as great. The book of Esther tells of the sinister plans hatched during the reign of king Xerxes to destroy the Jews throughout the Persian Empire. Esther's heroic intervention saved her people, an act still celebrated in modern times during the Jewish festival of Purim.

These seventeen documents make up the historical books of the Old Testament. They also provide a framework and a context for the five books of Old Testament poetry and the seventeen books of Old Testament prophecy. Every book of poetry falls chronologically under a portion of the history of the nation. Every book of prophecy fits chronologically within the sequence of the history of the nation. Once you have mastered the story of these books, you have come a long way toward understanding the Old Testament.

ABOUT ENJOYING THE BIBLE

In order to master the framework of this book, you will need to do the work suggested in the "Enjoying the Bible . . . " section of each chapter. Understanding and enjoyment go hand in hand. It is very difficult to enjoy that which you do not understand.

To help you grow in both understanding and enjoying the Bible, you will need to put into practice the exercises that will accompany each chapter of this book. The first of these exercises involves developing a plan for reading the Bible.

ENJOYING THE BIBLE: READING THE WORD

If you have not yet made this discovery, reading the Bible can be a life-changing experience. It has been in my life. Prior to my years as a university student, I had never read the Bible. Actually, I had attempted to read it on a number of occasions, but always seemed to get bogged down early in Genesis. It was somewhere around the tenth or eleventh *begat*, I believe.

Of course I decoded what *begat* meant from the context, but the word was certainly not part of my normal vocabulary. The King James Version was translated in 1611 when *begat* was a word used in everyday conversation. If you lived in that era, you spoke a version of English that sounded quite a bit different from the variety we speak in the twenty-first century. "How art thou?" would have been a normal greeting on the streets of Merry Old England.

For many years the King James Version was the only English bible available to the general population. Many people considered its language almost holy. The mindset was something like, "If the King James was good enough for the Apostle Paul, it's good enough for me." Obviously, Paul did not use the King James. Nor did anyone else before 1611, nor anyone after who did not speak English.

Most bibles around the world are translations of the Hebrew and Greek texts of the Old and New Testaments. The original Old Testament was written in Hebrew. The original New Testament was written in Greek. Sometimes you may hear a reference made to the "original manuscripts." We no longer possess these documents. Until 1948, the earliest texts of the Hebrew Old Testament available were dated around 1000 A.D. If you date the writing of the early books of the Old Testament at approximately 1500 B.C. — the time of Moses, traditional author of the first five books — then the earliest manuscripts were nearly 2,500 years removed from the originals. Critics of the Bible often pointed to this fact when asserting that no one could be sure that the Bible we have today has any continuity with the original.

To understand why this gap existed you need to know a few facts about textual transmission and the process of copying manuscripts. Before the advent of the printing press in the sixteenth century, all books were copied by hand. A class of Jewish scholars called scribes copied the scrolls of the Old Testament. Their task was considered a holy one. Before working on a scroll, they would ceremonially wash their hands. They often wore special garments and used special pens and quills for this sacred job.

One interesting detail of scribal work pertains to the name of God. Revealed to Moses in Exodus 3:14, the name of God held a special place of honor in the Jewish faith. Eventually, it was not even spoken, but read as "Lord" or "the Name" when texts containing the four-letter tetragrammaton (YHWH) were read publicly. In the process of copying a scroll, when the scribe came to the Name, he set down his pen, washed his hands, and then wrote with a special pen used only to copy God's name. Afterward, the scribe would place the special pen in its place, pick up his normal pen, and continue transcribing the text.

A complex system of checking for accuracy involved counting pages, paragraphs, sentences, and words to make sure the copy was exactly like the original. Here is where things get interesting. The finished product was so accurate it was considered superior to the original. And because it was thought that an old scroll could become worn and its words become unreadable, thus potentially producing error, the older copy was always destroyed upon completion of the new copy. As a result, no scrolls dating into antiquity survived. That is, until the discovery of the Dead Sea Scrolls.

In 1948, a Bedouin shepherd at the northern edge of the Dead Sea threw a rock into a cave to scare out a goat that had hidden there. When he heard the sound of something breaking and crawled inside to explore, he found the beginnings of one of the greatest archeological discoveries of the ages. He had broken a clay jar that contained fragments of ancient manuscripts.

This discovery led to major treasure hunts throughout the region, where many more jars with manuscript fragments were found. They had been hidden by a sect of Jewish ascetics known as the Essenes, who lived in the desert at the time of Christ. When the Roman legions marched on Jerusalem in 65 A.D., the Essenes began to hide their manuscripts in caves. Nearly two thousand years later, their scrolls would validate the incredible accuracy of Old Testament textual transmission.

In one swift discovery the gap between the originals of the Old Testament and the 1000 A.D. Masoretic texts was bridged. Manuscript could be compared against manuscript. The Dead Sea Scrolls contained at least partial fragments of every book in the Old Testament except Esther, and several complete scrolls of books such as Isaiah.

The result? Over a period of a thousand years, no major changes occurred that in any way would change or alter the meaning of the text. The only variations were slight stylistic changes as the Hebrew language changed over the years. The text had been miraculously preserved!

The New Testament documents have quite a different reason for generating our confidence. Like the Old Testament, the New Testament original manuscripts no longer exist. The earliest fragments we have of these documents are parts of the Gospel of John dating to around 117-125 A.D. The earliest complete texts we possess are second and third-century manuscripts.

How can we be sure that, like the Old Testament, the later texts accurately reflect the message of the originals? While we have very few early manuscripts of the Old Testament, we do possess a large number of manuscripts that can validate the New

Testament documents. Those who copied these texts held them in the same esteem that the scribes of Old Testament times did. But unlike the scribes, they did not destroy the old documents from which the new copies were made. Because the Bible was so rare, the old copies were kept and used as resources within the life of the early church. The result is that we now have thousands of copies of early New Testament documents to compare against each other.

However, this was not the case when the King James Version was translated. Most of the manuscripts we now possess are the product of recent archaeological discoveries. The King James was actually translated from a Latin version of the Bible called the Vulgate. The Vulgate itself was translated from the Hebrew and Greek by the early church father Jerome, who worked from extremely limited manuscript resources. Today scholars can actually produce a translation of the New Testament more faithful and accurate to the original than the translators of the King James could.

By comparing text against text, New Testament scholars have produced translations that most believe are at least 99 percent identical to the originals. Certainly, no major doctrine or point of history has been changed through the years. Bottom line: we can have complete confidence in modern translations of the Bible.

FINDING A BIBLE VERSION

This leads to my first "coaching tip": find a version that you like. You might have to experiment a bit to find the one that best fits your needs. When I first started reading the Bible as a college student, I used a paraphrase called *Good News for Modern Man*. At the time I didn't know that a paraphrase was different from a translation. A paraphrase takes an existing translation and attempts to make it more readable. It does not work from Greek or Hebrew texts, and pinpoint accuracy is not the objective.

To this day, one of my good friends reads another popular paraphrase, *The Living Bible*, which he jokingly calls "the linebacker's version." Although he has been to seminary, he prefers the simplicity of this version when reading the Bible.

I soon found myself wanting to be sure I was reading exactly what the original writers said, so I switched from my *Good New for Modern Man* to *The New American Standard Bible.* At the time, it was considered the most faithful to the ancient texts. I stayed with this version for many years until the New International Version (or NIV) came on the market. Attracted to it because its translators strove to maintain the accuracy of the New American Standard while making the language flow more like ordinary speech, it's the version I continue to use. A trip to a good religious bookstore will reveal many excellent versions to choose from. Find one that seems readable to you and buy it.

DEVELOPING A STRATEGY

The second coaching tip I would offer is this: develop a daily strategy. Begin this strategy by reading in the New Testament. When I started reading the Bible as a college student, I was pointed to the Gospel of John, a simple and beautiful account of the life of Christ. After reading John, I moved on to Luke, a highly detailed account of Jesus' life and ministry written by a physician. I compared it to John and found that they complemented each other without great repetition. In a later chapter, I will explain the differences of the four gospel accounts to you.

I then read the book of Acts, which records what happened after the resurrection and ascension of Jesus; a story of the first thirty years of the Christian church.

Next I moved on to the Apostle Paul's letters. Because of the way my mind works, I found these letters fascinating and read through all thirteen of them.

I read the entire New Testament before I tackled the Old. At the time, I did not know the history of the Old Testament or how it fit together. The first part of this chapter gives you a big jump on where I was when I began reading the Bible.

Let me suggest a few ways to develop a personal Bible- reading strategy:

1. *Read through the entire New Testament and Old Testament* once, in that order, like you were reading a novel. Get through it as fast as you can. It is not much longer than a big novel, and you might be surprised how easy this is to do.
2. After you have read through the entire Bible once, go back and begin to *read entire books, one at a time.* Many of the New Testament books are easy to read in one sitting. In a later chapter I am going to talk to you about using "tools" while you read. For now, just read.
3. *Set a goal to read at least five days a week.* Don't worry if you miss a day, but begin to develop a habit.
4. *Set aside a specific time daily to read.*
5. *Set aside a specific place to read.* Having a set time and place will help you solidify the habit.
6. Once you have read through the entire Bible and then reread it book by book, begin to set a goal to *slowly read one chapter a day.*

I believe that if you will develop this discipline, you will begin to enjoy the Bible like you never have in your life. I also believe this discipline will begin to have a direct impact on the quality of your spiritual life. This is a book like no other. In later chapters we will talk more about the devotional reading of the Bible, but for now, know this: God uses the Bible to speak to us personally. When we experience this phenomenon, we will understand why Bible reading has been a cornerstone of spiritual vitality throughout the centuries. It is a discipline you must develop if you are going to understand the Bible and enjoy it.

CHAPTER 2

The Poetic Books

§

A thorough knowledge of the Bible is worth
more than a college education.

— Theodore Roosevelt

Understanding Old Testament Poetry

With the final words of 2 Chronicles, the curtain falls on the historical books of the Old Testament. In the arrangement of documents in our English Bibles, the next section contains five books of Hebrew poetry. By designating these books as poetry, scholars have recognized that in the same way God used historical narrative to communicate his mind in the first seventeen books of the Old Testament, now he uses a different literary vehicle to tell his story.

The word *poetry* conjures many images in the minds of the Western thinker, most of them negative. Many of us men struggled through freshman English classes, attempting in vain to translate into prose what Dickinson, Frost, Blake, and others were trying to say.

Biblical poetry is not so obtuse. It *does* use imagery, metaphor, and simile to convey truth and typically is written in distinct grammatical form. But generally, the writers of Hebrew poetry, under inspiration of the Holy Spirit, communicated in ways that the least sophisticated among us can understand.

The five Old Testament books that we identify as poetry are Psalms, Proverbs, Ecclesiastes, Song of Solomon (or Song of Songs), and Job. Within these books, communication styles vary widely.

Job is written in the form of a stage play containing both historical narrative and poetic verse. The Psalms are lyrical songs, mostly used in the context of worship at the temple during the times of the United and Divided Kingdoms. Proverbs and Ecclesiastes are a style of Jewish writing known as wisdom literature. Proverbs contains a multitude of pithy observations on wise living, while Ecclesiastes is a more lengthy reflection on the nature of life itself. Finally, Song of Solomon is an epic love poem. It is one of the most sensuous pieces of literature from antiquity, yet throughout the ages it also has been recognized by both the Jewish and Christian faith communities as a metaphor of God's love for his people.

Let's take a look at each of these five books individually:

JOB

The account of Job is one of the Bible's better known stories. It is also one of the least understood. Most look at the book as the biblical explanation of why good people, even God's people, suffer. Yet Job may produce more frustration than clarity concerning mankind's eternal "why" question. Job is more of a non-answer, but one of extreme significance.

A surface reading of Job might lead one to assume that it should have been placed with the historical books rather than the poetic because it seems to be simply the narrative of a man whose life comes undone at the seams. A more careful analysis says otherwise, even though Jewish culture was not generally known for producing literature for the stage.

The book's first verse introduces us to Job, a good man who lives in the land of Uz. Biblical scholars confirm that nobody actually knows where Uz was (forgive the poetic observation!) or even if it ever existed. And so, most conclude that Job is possibly the oldest piece of literature in the Bible, preceding even the writings of Moses contained in Genesis through Deuteronomy.

God immediately calls Satan's attention to Job. "Have you seen this guy?!" (Job 1:8, Bob's loosely paraphrased version of the Old Testament). Satan responds with a challenge: "Sure he serves you. Why not? You've blessed his socks off!" (1:9-10, same translation). The implication is plain. "Dish out some hard times and see what the guy does." The gauntlet has been thrown down. God gives Satan permission to wreak havoc on Job and his family.

At this point, every reader of Job should become indignant. "Is God really like this? Does he arbitrarily let Satan cream us? And what in the world is Satan doing up there in his presence, anyway?" If the book of Job were purely historical narrative, these would be valid questions. But if Job is like a stage play based on historical reality, then we shouldn't ask questions until the play is over and we see how this all pans out. You have to admit, the playwright has our attention!

This introductory scene continues to build. Job is financially ruined and his children are annihilated. Still Job trusts God and lives in a spirit of relinquishment. The scene shifts back to heaven. (Try to imagine a stage where the heavenly action takes place on one side, while Job and the disasters occur on the other.) Satan again taunts and challenges God: "Big deal.

So you wiped him out. Get more personal and see what he does. Let me give him a few boils" (2:4-5, B ob's Loose Translation again). Again God gives permission for Job to be afflicted, but limits Satan's actions. With Job sitting on an ash heap, scraping the puss from his boils, Scene One draws to a close.

The bulk of the book revolves around a group of friends that comes to Job in his time of disaster and tries to make sense of the mess. Structurally, the middle chapters (chapters 3–37) contain three cycles of speeches, each highlighted by Job's response to his friends.

As you read these interactions, note the recurring themes. For one, Job's friends consistently argue, "Good things happen to good people; bad things happen to bad people." Although this was never the theology of the Scriptures, it was quite popular in ancient times and seems to persist even today in certain theological circles. In a fallen world, life is not fair.

After all the arguments have been presented, the climax of the book comes when heaven once again makes itself known. God himself confronts Job. It is here that most of us would hope a nice, clean answer to the problem of evil and pain would be offered. Instead God basically says to Job, "Who do you think you are — God? Where were you when I laid the earth's foundation?" (38:2-4, BLT again).

The message of the book of Job is that God is God. He doesn't need to explain himself. We probably couldn't understand if he did. Job gets it. Most readers of the book don't.

In the book's final scene Job's fortunes and family are restored. In the form of a play it all fits nicely. In real life it doesn't always happen that way. Life doesn't always make sense this side of Eden. That is the most important message of the book.

PSALMS

Job is followed in our English bibles by the book of Psalms. Like the Bible itself, Psalms is a collection of shorter works. The collection contains 150 sets of lyrics to songs used in Israel's worship at the Temple.

We often mistake the Psalms as being written exclusively by David. In reality David did write seventy-three of them. But other writers also contributed to the collection.

Eleven pieces were written by the "Sons of Korah", a title given to a group of Temple musicians both at the time of David and again at the time of Israel's return from captivity. Asaph, one of the chief musicians of the Temple, wrote twelve psalms. Individual psalms are attributed to men named Ethan and Heman. Both Solomon and Moses are given credit for composing one psalm each. Fifty of the psalms are of unknown authorship.

Each psalm is set in a historical context. Though not all these contexts are revealed to us, many psalms contain an introductory statement that tells us who wrote it, the occasion for writing, and the type of music that is to accompany the lyrics.

For example, Psalm 3 contains the introductory note, "A psalm of David. When he fled from his son Absalom." Knowing the history of David and Absalom will give new meaning to the psalm. Psalm 4 does not tell us the occasion, but notes, "With stringed instruments." Psalm 6 not only tells us what instruments were used to accompany the psalm, but also that it is, "According to *sheminith*." This term is thought to refer to the musical style of the song. This is also the case in Psalm 7 where the psalm is called, "A *shiggaion*."

Categories of the Psalms. The Psalms can be divided into a number of categories based on theme and structure. Some psalms are simple songs of thanksgiving and worship. For instance, Psalm 30 was written for the dedication of the Temple. It is filled with expressions of praise and thanksgiving for all God has done and exhortations to the people to sing and worship the Lord.

Others include confession of sin and pleas for forgiveness. The classic of this category is Psalm 51, written by David after his adulterous and murderous affair with Bathsheba. It is a song of repentance: "Have mercy on me, O God, according to your unfailing love" (verse 1).

Sometimes a psalm is a plea for help, often occasioned by the psalmist feeling overwhelmed by life's circumstances. You could view these psalms as the Jewish blues. Put a little blues vibe to your reading of the following: "Why are you downcast, O my soul? Why so disturbed within me?" (42:5).

One of the more fascinating themes of the Psalms is retribution. Theologians have labeled such psalms as "imprecatory"; they express heartfelt anger. For instance, Psalm 137 was written during Israel's exile in Babylon. The Babylonians apparently liked to twist the knife a bit by asking the Jews to sing some of the songs they were famous for. "Sing us one of the songs of Zion!" some Babylonian redneck demands (137:3). "Okay," says one of the circumcised guys. "Here's a little tune I wrote, but sorry, I'll have to sing it in Hebrew, which unfortunately you don't understand. This is my favorite verse." And he sings. "Happy is he who smashes your babies on the rocks" (137:8-9, BLT one last time).

Most of us never knew the Bible expressed this kind of sentiment. But realize that these songs are cries of the heart that express brutal honesty. They are a bit more refreshing than most of the religious drivel we have to put up with in our own times.

One other feature of the Psalms is worth noting. Hebrew poetry was often structured grammatically. If you read the marginal notes in your Bible, periodically you will find that a particular psalm is an alphabetical acrostic. This means that the psalm is composed in such a way that the first word in each succeeding verse or section begins with the next succeeding letter of the Hebrew alphabet.

The longest psalm in the Bible is Psalm 119. Notice that its 176 verses are divided into twenty-two sections, each labeled with one of the twenty-two letters of the Hebrew alphabet. In this psalm, which is an epic ballad lauding the value of God's Word, the first word in each line of each section begins with the section letter. Each succeeding section continues this pattern with the next letter of the Hebrew alphabet.

PROVERBS

The third book of biblical "poetry" is Proverbs. A proverb is simply a wise saying. The book of Proverbs is a compilation of these wise sayings, primarily collected from the writings of Solomon, King of Israel. You might remember that early in Solomon's reign God gave him the opportunity to ask for anything he wished. Solomon requested wisdom to govern Israel. In response, God granted him a measure of wisdom that has never been equaled, apart from Jesus.

Wisdom differs from knowledge. Knowledge involves the mastery of information; wisdom involves the mastery of life. The Hebrew word *hokmah* (or *hakam*), translated "wise" or "wisdom," means "skill in living." Two of my favorite definitions of wisdom are "the ability to distinguish that which is trivial from that which is fundamental" and "the ability to see life from God's point of view."

Proverbs contains thirty-one chapters of short, pithy observations and instructions concerning how to live life well. The opening verses of the book summarize its intent:

For attaining wisdom and discipline;
for understanding words of insight;
for acquiring a disciplined and prudent life, doing what is right
and just and fair;
for giving prudence to the simple,
knowledge and discretion to the young. (1:2-4)

Because the Hebrew culture was extremely pragmatic in its faith, it is not surprising that the book of Proverbs is thematically structured around a number of archetypal characters. Proverbs teaches its lessons by painting word pictures of these characters. We see the actions of a particular character and how those actions affect his life.

There are ten central characters in the book, the pre- dominant of which are the wise man and the fool. The wise man is the one who possesses and exercises wisdom. The fool is the one who does not. A typical contrast of these two can be found in Proverbs 10:14 where we are told: "Wise men store up knowledge, but the mouth of a fool invites ruin."

Another pair of contrasting characters are the righteous man and the wicked. In this same Proverb (verse 20) we read: "The tongue of the righteous is choice silver, but the heart of the wicked is of little value."

Other contrasts include the diligent man and the lazy man, the naïve or simple person and the prudent person, and the honorable wife and the adulteress. Less-central characters are the kind man and the cruel man, and the generous man and the stingy man.

As this collection of wise sayings was passed from one generation to the next, it became a way of instilling values. I have often imagined that these truths were used in the process of male initiation. Their transmission was intended to ensure that Israel's position as a nation built on solid spiritual values would endure.

ECCLESIASTES

The fourth of the poetic books is another piece of wisdom literature. Attributed to king Solomon, it is a record of his reflections on the fact that nothing in life brings lasting satisfaction but God. The line that repeatedly occurs through- out the book is "vanity of vanities, all is vanity" (KJV). More contemporary versions translate this classic phrase as "Meaningless! Meaningless! Everything is meaningless."

One of the remarkable dimensions of Ecclesiastes is its modern relevance. The expression "Nothing new under the sun" actually comes from this book (1:9). Solomon's pursuits in his culture are often the very same pursuits in which we find ourselves engaged.

Solomon pursued knowledge. He tells us, "I devoted myself to study and to explore by wisdom all that is done under heaven" (1:13). For an age and culture where often a Ph.D. is viewed as G-O-D, Solomon makes a profoundly relevant assessment: "With much wisdom comes much sorrow; the more knowledge, the more grief" (1:18). His pursuit of learning was "meaningless, a chasing after the wind" (1:14).

Solomon also pursued hedonism. The primary difference between Solomon and the typical American male was his ability to pursue pleasure without the restrictions of a limited budget. Solomon said, "I thought in my heart, 'Come now, I will test you with pleasure to find out what is good'" (2:1). With seven hundred wives, three hundred concubines, and an annual income in the six billion dollar range (which went a great deal further in 1000 B.C., nontaxable dollars!), he had the resources to go for the gusto! But his assessment of this lifestyle was equally bleak: "But that also proved to be meaningless" (2:1).

Our modern, materially driven culture measures success by the number and value of our possessions — cars, houses, clothes, watches, and recreational toys. Solomon tried to achieve satisfaction in this way too, acquiring houses, vineyards, gardens, parks, orchards, slaves, herds, flocks, silver, and gold. Perhaps his accomplishments in this area are best summarized when he says, "I denied myself nothing my eyes desired" (2:10).

Few of us have the ability to make such a statement (though many of us wish we could!). Again, Solomon's assessment of his vast possessions was, "Yet when I surveyed all that my hands had done and what I had toiled to achieve, everything was meaningless, a chasing after the wind" (2:11).

While Ecclesiastes may be difficult to understand at times, its conclusion is quite clear. The wisest, richest, most powerful man of the Old Testament sums it all up with a simple challenge, "Now all has been heard; here is the conclusion of the matter: Fear God and keep his commandments" (12:13).

SONG OF SOLOMON

The final book of Old Testament poetry is known by several different titles. It is sometimes called "The Song of Songs". At other times it is called "Canticles", a word meaning "songs." Frequently the title used is "Song of Solomon". All these titles are derived from the first line of the text, which informs us that this is "the song of songs, which is Solomon's" (NASB).

The Song of Solomon is a hotly debated book, for at its most obvious level of understanding it is a sensual tribute to romantic love. Because of this, throughout history some have questioned its inclusion in the canon. Historically, it received its place because it was thought to be an allegory of God's love for his people. It is most likely both.

At its most natural, the Song is an epic love poem written in honor of Solomon and the most recent of his many wives. In vivid language and imagery it describes the growing passion and longing between the lover and his bride. "My lover is mine and I am his," reflects the overarching theme (2:16).

At various times in history, scholars and churchmen have had difficulty embracing the book at this level. The creeping Gnosticism of the early church and the blatantly negative view of women that developed both in Jewish and early church history were hard to reconcile with the Song of Solomon.

Verses such as "I am a wall, and my breasts are like towers" must have put some ascetic monks into cardiac arrest! (8:10). It was during these years that the more allegorical or symbolic interpretation of the piece grew in popularity.

As an allegory or metaphor, the book paints a picture of God as the great lover and his people as the beloved. We see in the allegory how God passionately pursues his people. We also see something of how God desires that his people respond to him with the same passion.

Mystics have long pointed out that there is a "knowing" relationship so intimate that sexual union is the only appropriate metaphor. Indeed, in the book of Genesis, *know* was the word used to speak of Adam's sexual union with Eve (Genesis 4:1, KJV).

The symbolic or allegorical understanding of the book sees the many obstacles and difficulties the lovers encounter as images of the challenges of obtaining and maintaining intimacy with God. Why not read the book carefully and reflectively and come to your own conclusions?

ENJOYING THE BIBLE: HEARING THE WORD

Enjoying the Bible involves the practice of several spiritual disciplines. It would be my guess that many men and women hear the Bible long before they ever read it. Most of us first hear the Bible in church.

From the time I was in elementary school until I was nearly out of college, I did not attend church. But when I seriously began looking at the claims of Christ, I went to hear Dr. Ted Nissan of Colonial Presbyterian Church in Kansas City, Missouri, explain how the Bible applies to our daily lives. I found Ted's messages so compelling that for the first time in my life I waited with eager anticipation for Sunday mornings. As a skeptical "child of the '60s," this newfound excitement about church surprised even me.

Jim Rayburn, founder of Young Life, once said, "It is a sin to bore a kid with Christ." His reasoning was that because Jesus Christ is the most exciting person who ever lived, knowing and following him should be an adventure. If we take the person of Christ and the Christian life and turn it into a boring drudgery, we have done God — and ourselves — a great disservice!

I would modify Rayburn's quote by saying, "It is a sin to bore anyone with the Bible." This is the greatest book in the world. This is God's book. This is a book that contains a message from the living God to his beloved children. This is a book that shows us what life is all about. This is a book where we can actually encounter God through the activity of his Spirit as we hear it and read it. How tragic that some men and women have the uncanny ability to make it boring!

We need to hear the Bible. "Faith comes from hearing," according to Romans 10:17. There is something that happens in the physiological process of hearing that affects a different part of our brain than that which is affected by reading the Bible. So here is my first coaching tip about enjoying the Bible by hearing the Bible: *Find a place where someone is teaching the Bible in a way that motivates you to come again and again to hear the Word of God.*

The most logical place for this to happen is a church. Unfortunately, this is not always the case. Many churches today don't use the Bible. These are often churches led by men or women who have gone to seminary to study to become ministers and tragically left seminary with their faith shattered. They have been trained in humanistic approaches to religion that are devoid of biblical truth. They have nothing to offer their congregations but platitudes garbed in religious language.

If you don't regularly attend church, and you decide to give it a try after reading this book, make sure the churches you visit use the Bible. Let me give you one idea of how to find out if a specific church is one where you can actually hear the Word. Call the church office and ask what the minister will be speaking on this Sunday. If the answer is something like, "The Social Consciousness of the Modern Dilemma," hang up and call another. Don't waste your time on a visit.

If they say, "How to Build a Healthy Family," you might want to give it a try and see what's up. Sometimes this can be good; sometimes this can be weak. There is a big trend today for churches to be "seeker friendly" and attempt to use Sunday morning services as more of a time for evangelism than for teaching the Bible. Often in these churches some other venue exists where you can go and actually "hear" the Word.

If, when you call, the person on the other end says something like, "Our pastor is preaching through the book of Ephesians. This Sunday he will be speaking on the second chapter": Go! This is what you are looking for.

Another place to hear the Bible is at a Bible study. Check around to see if a good one is being taught in your area. I currently teach a midweek study in the Denver area for men and women who are looking for more biblical instruction. You'll likely discover a study or two like this in your neck of the woods as well.

How to Hear

It might seem strange to talk about how to hear. Isn't this a natural process when we get ourselves in position to listen to a speaker? Studies suggest this is not the case. At a recent communications workshop I learned that exit surveys taken at churches around the country indicated that 86 percent of those leaving church could not tell the person taking the survey the main point of the message. Although exit surveys are not always absolutely accurate, these would seem to indicate that the people in the pews had been hearing but not listening. Amazingly, the same researchers surveyed the pastors who had given the messages at these churches and found that 16 percent of the pastors could not articulate the main point of the message they had just delivered. "Hello, Houston . . . "

I have often reflected on how other cultures have honed the art of hearing to a fine skill. Many of the cultures of antiquity — which we mistakenly call "uncivilized" today — did not or do not have written language. In cultures where written language does not exist, oral communication becomes the means by which the entire history and value system of the culture is transmitted. Research into these cultures has revealed that the accuracy of transmission and retention is remarkably high.

Some of you may remember Alex Haley's epic tale, *Roots*. The story depicted how generation after generation passed on their heritage orally. Such was likely the case in the early days of biblical history. Moses is usually given credit for authorship of the first five books of the Bible. If this is true, it is clear that much of his material was passed along in oral form for generations before being written down.

Many men and women in our contemporary world could use some help in being better listeners. We know this is true in our homes, families, and marriages, but it is also true when we sit to listen to the Bible. We need to become more effective listeners. How do we do that? Let me make a few suggestions:

1. *Make your listening intentional.* Go to church with the mindset of a learner and a listener. Know that when the service is over you are going to test yourself to see how much you remember.

2. *Take notes.* Many churches today recognize that the old way of preaching did not always get the job done. Learning theorists tell us that nearly 85 percent of what we hear we forget within three hours. This figure rises to 95 percent by the end of twenty-four hours. If this is the case, no wonder most churchgoers don't have a clue what they just heard. Taking notes adds several more learning resources to your listening. You are actively listening when you take notes. Your body is involved in listening. You are moving

and writing and you are visually interacting with the material. When I teach I always try to encourage my listeners to take notes. When I teach, I also use Keynote to "force" my audience to *see* as well as *hear* what I am saying.

Many pastors include some kind of sermon outline in the bulletin. This helps their congregations more clearly follow their train of thought. If you asked these pastors what they have just attempted to communicate, they can usually tell you clearly and succinctly. The discipline of making an outline forces us to focus our thoughts.

3. *Talk to someone about what you have just heard.* Interaction reinforces hearing. Dialogue with another listener also can clarify. Someone has said, "To speak is to be misunderstood." I am always amazed at what I hear someone has said that I said. Try to get with someone after your "Bible hearing" event and discuss the material immediately afterward.

4. *Review your notes.* Sit down later in the day or the next day and go over your notes. Attempt to remember what you have heard.

5. *Talk about what you have heard with someone not present at the event.* Use conversation as a tool to articulate what you have heard. "Hey, you know what Ed said at church yesterday?" This can be an exciting exercise when you are around friends and coworkers who did not make it to a "hearing event" like you did!

6. *Learn to listen for the "other voice."* When you are listening to the Bible, it is not only the speaker speaking. God uses these encounters to speak through the speaker. The Holy Spirit has the ability to take what has been generically prepared for an entire audience and personalize it

to your needs. I can't tell you how many times people have asked me if someone told me about what was going on in their lives before I spoke. Somehow God had used what I said to speak directly to them. You have to put on another set of "ears" to pick up this message. It is always the most important message, and it is too bad so many miss it by not knowing how to hear the Word.

CHAPTER 3

The Prophets

§

The Bible is a letter from Almighty God to His creatures.

— St. Gregory the Great

Understanding the Prophets

The third major division of the Bible contains the writings of the Old Testament prophets. The prophetic writings include seventeen books that are usually divided into two subsections. The first five books, as organized in the English Bible, are referred to as the Major Prophets. The remaining twelve are called the Minor Prophets.

At first glance, we might assume that these designations refer to the significance of the content. Actually, the designations primarily refer to the fact that the Major Prophets are lengthy books, whereas the Minor Prophets are relatively short ones. The one book that does not fit this criterion is Lamentations, found in the middle of the Major Prophets. Although short, it is so intimately connected to the book of Jeremiah that its placement with the Major Prophets makes a great deal of sense.

Note the symmetry of the prophetic book structure with that of the historical books. Each section contains seventeen books. Both sections are structured with five primary books followed by twelve secondary writings. Recognizing and remembering patterns like this can help you keep a handle on how the Bible fits together.

THE MAJOR PROPHETS

ISAIAH

Though some critics believe the book of Isaiah contains two distinct works — one written by a later author referred to as Second Isaiah — the history of biblical scholarship still leans toward the integrity and unity of the book and its single authorship. When you see the overview of the work, I believe you will come to the same conclusion.

The primary reason many critics suggest two authors has to do with the radically different tone of the first and second halves of the book. The first half is filled with prophetic declarations of God's coming judgment, the second half with messages of hope. A distinct change does take place after chapter 39. But rather than viewing this as a proof of two authors, I believe the two themes reflect the two messages of the entire Bible: law and grace. The first thirty-nine chapters are filled with warnings of God's judgment on Israel for its sin. The final twenty-seven chapters are promises of God's never-ending love and grace. This second section contains some of the greatest prophecies of the coming of Christ.

Each of the prophetic books sits in a historical context that creates the background for the book. Knowing the background is a major factor in understanding the prophet's message and its application both in its original setting and for the contemporary audience. Usually, the setting can be found in the opening lines of the book.

The opening verses of Isaiah tell us that Isaiah ministered during the reigns of four Old Testament kings of Israel: Uzziah, Jotham, Ahaz, and Hezekiah. This places the book chronologically at around 750 to 700 B.C. This information also tells us that Isaiah was primarily a prophet to the Southern Kingdom of Judah, though he did live during the invasion and destruction of the Northern Kingdom of Israel in 722 B.C. He prophesied the disaster coming on the North and then lived to see the prophecy fulfilled.

In a sense, the book of Isaiah is like a mini-model of the entire Bible. It contains sixty-six chapters, just as the Bible contains sixty-six books. Just as the thirty-nine books of the Old Testament are filled with Israel's failure, ending with the destruction of Jerusalem, the first thirty-nine chapters of Isaiah are filled with the same theme of judgment.

Isaiah begins by warning both Israel and Judah of their sin and of God's judgment if they do not change. It is interesting to see that during Isaiah's ministry both good kings *and* bad kings ruled the Southern kingdom (under Hezekiah and Josiah, Judah experienced wonderful revival). During this same period, only bad kings ruled the North. Within twenty years of the time Isaiah started his ministry, the Northern kingdom ceased to exist.

In chapters 11–39, Isaiah delivers a series of messages of coming judgment to other nations. Even the nations of Assyria and Babylon, used by God to discipline Israel and Judah, become subjects of Isaiah's message.

In the same way that the final twenty-seven books of the Bible contain the New Covenant, or Testament, of God's fulfilled grace in the person of Jesus, the second section of Isaiah is filled with messianic prophecies of the very events portrayed in the New Testament.

With the first words of chapter 40 we sense a shift has taken place: "Comfort, comfort my people, says your God" (40:1). The focus of this hope is the promise of the coming Messiah. One chapter that illustrates this focus is Isaiah 53. Here you will find one of the most amazing pictures of Christ's coming in all the Old Testament: "We all, like sheep, have gone astray, each of us has turned to his own way; and the Lord has laid on him [Jesus] the iniquity of us all" (53:6).

Isaiah is a marvelous piece of biblical literature. Jesus must have loved it, for he quoted more from this Old Testament book than from any other.

JEREMIAH

The opening verses of Jeremiah tell us that Jeremiah was the son of a priest of Israel. We also learn that he was from the region of Benjamin, just to the north of Judah. his prophetic ministry began in the thirteenth year of king Josiah's reign and lasted through the fall of Jerusalem. he spoke to the Southern kingdom during its darkest days, and his message was so bleak that he is often referred to as "the weeping prophet." His was the final warning to the people of Judah before their conquest and destruction by the Babylonian Empire.

One characteristic of many of the prophetic books is the tension between impending disaster and future hope. Jeremiah follows this pattern, depicting both scathing indictment of Judah's sin and promise of healing and restoration for the nation.

In the midst of the nation's judgment by exile, Daniel read the words of Jeremiah and understood that the captivity in Babylon was to last seventy years. This truth motivated Daniel to pray, and in response the angel Gabriel was sent to him with the timetable of the next five hundred years of Israel's history (Daniel 9:20-27).

It was Jeremiah who gave the message that a day was coming when the struggle Israel experienced because of its failure to keep the Law would end. The Old Covenant would be replaced by a new covenant, one in which God would write his law on human hearts and forgive humanity's sin (31:31-34). These promises form the Old Testament background to Jesus' words in the Upper Room, when he informed the disciples that the bread and cup they partook of were symbols of his sacrifice for mankind. The New Covenant, promised by Jeremiah, was about to be inaugurated.

LAMENTATIONS

The middle book of the Major Prophets does not actually meet the criterion to qualify as a "major" prophet. Lamentations is not a lengthy book, containing just five chapters. But it is placed at this point in our Bible both because it is the continuation of Jeremiah's previous work and because it provides a bridge between the prophecies given before the fall of Jerusalem and the two major prophets who wrote during Judah's captivity.

Lamentations is Jeremiah's lament over the destroyed city of Jerusalem. The lament begins, "How deserted lies the city, once so full of people!" (1:1). In our study of the historical books, we saw that the Babylonian conquest of Judah consisted of several phases. Most scholars date the initial conquest at 607 B.C. when Babylon actually took control. As was typical of the Babylonian approach to a conquered people, they transported the leadership of the nation to Babylon to indoctrinate them in Babylonian culture while establishing a mock, indigenous government in the conquered territory.

Zedekiah, the puppet king installed by the Babylonians, began to believe he could enlist the help of Egypt to overthrow the captors. His rebellion led Nebuchadnezzar to move to "plan B" of the subjugation strategy. The Babylonian army marched on Jerusalem and put it under siege. The siege lasted two years, cutting off the city from any outside provision. The situation became so desperate that women began to eat their own babies in stark starvation and desperation (Lamentations 2:20). Finally, between 587 and 586 B.C. the Babylonians torched the city and destroyed the temple.

Amazingly, in the midst of this absolute disaster is a well-known message of hope and a demonstration of Jeremiah's trust in God: "Because of the Lord's great love we are not consumed, for his compassions never fail. They are new every morning; great is your faithfulness" (3:22-23).

EZEKIEL

Ezekiel is the prophet most likely not to have been chosen to serve on your church's staff. He was either a relatively weird bird or God asked him to do some very strange things. Either way, he stands among the Major Prophets with a message of both judgment and hope.

Like Daniel, Ezekiel was a prophet of the captivity. Unlike Daniel, he was not taken to be with Judah's elite but ministered among the exiles themselves in the land of Babylon. In fact, he received his vision in a refugee camp along the banks of an irrigation canal called the Kebar River.

Ezekiel's message is divided into three parts, the first of which concerns the destruction of Jerusalem found in the first twenty-four chapters. One of the unique qualities of the book of Ezekiel is the visionary form his prophecy takes. His experience has many parallels to that of the apostle John on the island of Patmos, where the resurrected and glorified Christ appeared and gave the Revelation.

Ezekiel started prophesying at the very time Zedekiah was being encouraged by false prophets in Judah to rebel against the Babylonians. Ezekiel told of the coming disaste. His message was simple: "The end! The end has come" (7:2). Many of the reasons for the severity of Judah's judgment are explained in Ezekiel. The nation was filled with idols, the leaders had led the people astray, and the prophets had spoken falsely. The glory had departed from Israel.

Like Isaiah's, this book's prophetic message is not limited to Judah. Its second section (chapters 25–35) contains messages to the nations surrounding Judah. Even mighty Egypt will not escape the judgment of God.

Also, like Isaiah and Jeremiah, Ezekiel ends with a message of hope. The final chapters deal with Judah's future return out of exile and its restoration. Ezekiel is famous for his vision of the valley of Dry Bones (37:1-14), a picture of the nation's rebirth.

The prophet also speaks of the end times. Daniel and Revelation both tie into the messages of the final chapters of this fascinating book.

Finally, Ezekiel transcends even the end times of this age and gives visions of a restored temple and nation that many believe fit in the scenario of the age to come.

DANIEL

One of the young leaders of Jerusalem taken into Babylonian exile was Daniel. His writings comprise the fifth and final book of the Major Prophets. In some ways, Daniel's words fit our more common understanding of prophecy. Rather than being one who denounced sin, Daniel was a visionary whom God used to reveal future plans and purposes for Israel.

The book of Daniel contains some of the most commonly known stories of the Old Testament. Almost every child has heard of Daniel in the lions' den (chapter 6). Or of Shadrach, Meshach, and Abednego and their deliverance from the fiery furnace (chapter 3). What is less commonly known are Daniel's visions and dreams concerning future events.

Daniel is an apocalyptic visionary. As such, his book is closely related to the New Testament book of Revelation, which finds its roots in the visions of Daniel. Here we see beasts and horns and dragons and wild animals. All symbolically represent kingdoms and kings and stages of human history.

With precise accuracy, Daniel unveils the coming empires that will occupy the world's center stage. The precision of the text is so amazing that skeptical scholars postulated that it was written *ex post facto*. More recent scholarship has challenged these allegations and again confirmed the integrity of the original text.

Daniel's primary message is that a time is coming when the kingdoms of man will crumble. Some will be conquered by other human kingdoms, but ultimately the kingdom of God and of the Son of Man will fill the whole earth. Daniel is the prophet of the coming messianic king and his kingdom.

One of the most fascinating sections of Daniel is chapter 9. While reading the words of the prophet Jeremiah and understanding that the captivity was to last seventy years, Daniel prayed for the nation. In response, he received a visitation from the angel Gabriel, who revealed that "seventy sevens" had been decreed for the people of Daniel. These seventy sevens refer to seventy periods of seven years. The trigger of this timetable would be a decree to rebuild and restore Jerusalem. Most scholars of the prophetic books believe this is a reference to the decree issued by the Persian ruler Artaxerxes in 445 B.C.

The prophecy speaks of seven sevens, or forty-nine years, for Jerusalem to be rebuilt. Then, after sixty-two sevens, or 434 years, the Messiah would come, the Messiah would be rejected, and Jerusalem would once again be destroyed. This would leave one final "seven." This final seven-year period is to be triggered by a ruler who will come and enter into a covenant with the nation Israel. This covenant will initiate the seventieth and final seven or "week" of human history.

Forty-nine years after the decree by Artaxerxes, the city of Jerusalem had been rebuilt with walls and the temple. Four-hundred-thirty-four years later, Jesus Christ entered Jerusalem on what we now call Palm Sunday. Five days later he was "cut off" by crucifixion. The timetable was remark- ably accurate.

We live in the days before the seventieth week. This final period of history is what John writes of in the book of Revelation, to be climaxed by the second coming of Jesus Christ.

THE MINOR PROPHETS

Twelve prophetic writings fall within the category of the Minor Prophets. There is little logic to their order and each requires a bit of background knowledge to understand its message. Your grasp of the historical material in chapter 1 of this book will help you better master the message of these particular Old Testament books.

HOSEA

The first book of the Minor Prophets is Hosea. Hosea prophesied during the reigns of Uzziah, Jotham, Ahaz, and Hezekiah, kings of Judah, and also during the reign of Jeroboam of Israel. This information gives us the time of the prophet, his audience, and — by knowing the historical situation of that period — a glimpse into what prompted the message. It also tells us that Hosea was a contemporary of Isaiah. Hosea is instructed by God to become a living object lesson to an unfaithful nation by marrying a woman who was a whore, or prostitute. God uses this scandalous situation to show the nation how he views their spiritual adultery and rebellion.

As if this situation weren't bad enough, Hosea's wife deserts him, painting yet another picture of how God views Israel's infidelity. Then God tells Hosea to go and find his strayed whore of a wife and take her back. What an incredible illustration of God's mercy and grace!

JOEL

Though the book of Joel follows Hosea, chronologically we believe Joel preceded Hosea by about a decade. Joel's primary message was directed to the Southern kingdom of Judah. His message was again one of judgment and hope.

Joel is unique in its portrait of how the nation's continued stubbornness resulted in successive waves of discipline. God's correction was to come in the form of both human and natural enemies.

One of the better-known sections of the book is Joel's vision of the locusts. As a plague of locusts devours the land, so God has allowed his nation to be ravaged. What one invader has left behind, the next has devoured. Wave after wave of invaders move across the nation. But God's promise in the midst of these horrors is that a day is coming when he will restore what the locust has eaten.

Joel is probably best known for his vision of the end times: "And afterward, I will pour out my Spirit on all people" (2:28). This prophecy was partially fulfilled at Pentecost when Peter explained the outpouring of the Holy Spirit by saying, "This is what was spoken by the prophet Joel" (Acts 2:16).

This prophecy will find its ultimate fulfillment and consummation at the second coming of Christ.

AMOS

Amos was not a known prophet but a shepherd whom God called to a prophetic ministry. A contemporary of Hosea, Amos prophesied during the reigns of Uzziah and Jeroboam around 785 B.C. Amos's most famous prophetic exclamation is, "Let justice roll down like waters" (5:24, NASB). His indictment of the nation is for the way their spiritual unfaithfulness has been expressed in social injustice. God will discipline the nation and send them into exile for their sin. Like Hosea and Joel, the message ends with a promise of regathering and restoration.

OBADIAH

Obadiah is one of the two minor prophets who did not bring a message for either Israel or Judah. Obadiah's prophecy concerns Edom. Because we are not given a historical reference point in the text, it is hard to date the message with a high degree of accuracy, but the content has led scholars to place it around the time of the destruction of Jerusalem in 587 B.C.

The Edomites were perennial enemies of Israel. They seemed to oppose the nation whenever they had a chance. They resisted the original exodus into the land of Canaan and tended to ally themselves with whatever army was invading the country. One significant example of this pattern is found in Psalm 137:7. One of the psalms written from captivity in Babylon, the psalmist calls on God to "Remember, O Lord, what the Edomites did on the day Jerusalem fell. 'Tear it down,' they cried, 'tear it down to its foundations!'" Now, Obadiah has a message for them regarding their future: "As you have done, it will be done to you" (Obadiah 15). Unlike the messages of previous prophets, there are no words of hope for Edom.

JONAH

The book of Jonah is probably the best known of all the Minor Prophets. It is not primarily a message *given by* the prophet, but rather a message *about* the prophet.

Jonah was the reluctant prophet sent to Nineveh, the capital of the Assyrian Empire, about 140 years before the Assyrians destroyed the Northern kingdom. Jonah did not want to go, so he hopped a boat and headed in the opposite direction. He was the prototypical modern man — running from God.

God "prepared a fish" for Jonah, but it was not for dinner. Actually, Jonah *was* dinner. He became human sushi. The Hebrew here does not mean "whale," but merely "large fish." Inside this fish, Jonah had a change of heart. He repented of his disobedience and was vomited up by the fish on the shores of guess where? Nineveh!

Jonah proclaimed his message to Nineveh and, unlike the response to the other prophets, the people actually listened and repented. God spared Nineveh. Ironically, Jonah responded to God's mercy by becoming depressed and desiring to die. The book's final encounter between God and Jonah shows the love and mercy of God for all people, not just the Jews. This is a remarkable book for the Jewish people to include in their Scriptures and a good illustration of the providential work of God in shaping the canon.

MICAH

The next book of the Minor Prophets not only tells us the time in which the prophet ministered but the specific audience and objective of his message. Micah prophesied during the reigns of Jotham, Ahaz, and Hezekiah, roughly around 750 B.C. God gave him a vision concerning "Samaria and Jerusalem." Samaria was the capital of the Northern kingdom of Israel, and Jerusalem was the capital of the Southern kingdom of Judah.

In the midst of a dismal message of judgment, Micah is known for prophesying two rays of hope. One is the message that one day the nations of the world will enjoy peace: "They will beat their swords into plowshares and their spears into pruning hooks" (4:3).

The second is a prophecy of the coming Messiah in which Micah tells his listeners where to look for the Christ: "But you, Bethlehem Ephrathah, though you are small among the clans of Judah, out of you will come for me one who will be ruler over Israel, whose origins are from of old, from ancient times" (5:2).

NAHUM

Nahum is the second book in the Minor Prophets that carried a message not specifically intended for either the Northern or the Southern kingdoms. Like Obadiah, who spoke against Israel's adversary Edom, Nahum addressed his message to the Assyrian Empire. The content of the message has led scholars to date it sometime after the destruction of the Northern kingdom by the Assyrians in 722 B.C.

Speaking decades after Jonah saw the people of Nineveh repent, Nahum sends a message of total devastation for the Assyrian Empire: "Nothing can heal your wound; your injury is fatal" (3:19).

HABAKKUK

Not much is known about the prophet Habakkuk or the specific circumstances under which his message was given. A reference to the Babylonians (1:6) makes us think that the date of the work is around 625 B.C., after the destruction of the Northern Kingdom and before the defeat of the Assyrians by the Babylonians in 612 B.C.

The message of Habakkuk is general enough to apply to almost any historical period. It begins with the prophet's complaint against God, asking why he allows so much injustice without intervening. God answers: "Look at the nations and watch — and be utterly amazed. For I am going to do something in your days that you would not believe, even if you were told" (1:5). What follows this verse is God's promise to bring judgment on Israel through the Babylonian Empire.

God responds to Habakkuk's second complaint by issuing a series of "woes." He condemns immorality, idolatry, wealth gained by extortion, a realm built by unjust gain, and a city built with bloodshed.

Habakkuk contains two brief passages more commonly known than the book in general. In contrast to the wickedness of the majority, God reminds his people that "the righteous will live by . . . faith" (2:4). This truth will become the cornerstone of much New Testament theology, specifically quoted by Paul in his arguments in Galatians 3:11.

The second well-known passage comes at the end of the book, where the prophet speaks of how God has made "my feet like the feet of a deer, he enables me to go on the heights" (3:19).

ZEPHANIAH

Zephaniah was a contemporary of Habakkuk, prophesying to the Southern kingdom during the reign of Josiah, king of Judah. By this time the Northern kingdom lies desolate. Zephaniah speaks of the Day of the Lord in this short book, picturing it as a day of distress that will come upon Judah. He also issues judgments against Moab, Ammon, Cush, and Assyria.

The third chapter of the book is an indictment specifically directed against Jerusalem and even more specifically against Judah's leaders. Zephaniah calls the rulers and officials "wolves" and "lions." He describes the official prophets as "arrogant" and "treacherous," and he points the finger at the priests for profaning their holy office.

Like the pattern in many of the prophets, Zephaniah ends with a message of hope. God will restore the fortunes of his people. One day, their punishment will be taken away and the Lord himself will be in their midst as a victorious warrior who will love and delight over them.

THE RESTORATION PROPHETS

The final three minor prophets ministered during the period of Judah's restoration. Placing them within the context of the historical books, they speak after the Southern kingdom has been conquered by the Babylonians in 587 B.C. The messages of the previous prophets have proven true. God has done just as he said. But just as he has judged, now he will restore.

Jeremiah had said the captivity would last seventy years, and Daniel had received a word from God that verified this message. When king Cyrus of Persia defeated the Babylonians, he issued a decree in 538 B.C., exactly seventy years after the initial conquest of Judah, declaring that whoever wished could return to Jerusalem to rebuild the temple. This marked the beginning of the Restoration Period. Again, remember how the historical books of Ezra and Nehemiah deal with this period and give the background to these three prophets. The restoration lasted nearly 150 years and took place in three phases. First the temple was rebuilt; next the walls of the city were restored; and finally the people themselves were spiritually renewed through the ministry of Ezra and prophets like Haggai, Zechariah, and Malachi.

HAGGAI

The first of the restoration prophets was Haggai. Haggai received a message from God on "the first day of the sixth month" of the second year of the reign of king Darius (1:1). This tells us that the book begins in 520 B.C. It also alerts us to the fact that it has been sixteen years since the work on the temple started under Cyrus's directive.

Going back to the book of Ezra, we are reminded how the neighboring peoples of Jerusalem opposed the project and effectively brought work on the temple to a standstill. What we don't pick up without knowing these dates is that the "pause" lasted sixteen years! It was at this point that God sent Haggai to light a fire.

The message of Haggai can be summarized by these words he spoke for God to the people: "Consider your ways!" (1:5,7, NASB). It seems that a legitimate reason to stop building had become a convenient excuse by this time. People were focusing on their own personal needs and not giving the temple project the priority it deserved. The results were classic: "You have planted much, but have harvested little. You eat, but never have enough. . . . You put on clothes, but are not warm. You earn wages, only to put them in a purse with holes in it" (1:6).

In what is one of the most successful missions of an Old Testament prophet, the people actually responded to Haggai's message. On the twenty-fourth day of the sixth month, only three weeks after the first message, they returned to work on the temple. The second temple was completed and dedicated in 516 B.C.

ZECHARIAH

Zechariah's message is one of the more symbolic among the Minor Prophets. His visions of horns and plumb lines, flying scrolls, and golden lampstands are reminiscent of portions of Daniel and Ezekiel. The message contains the kind of apocalyptic imagery we will find later in the New Testament book of Revelation.

A contemporary of Haggai, Zechariah begins by telling us that "the word of the Lord" came to him in the eighth month of the second year of Darius. Like Haggai, this would place the message in 520 B.C. Also like Haggai, part of Zechariah's mission was to motivate the people to rebuild the temple. Zechariah does this by revealing the future of this temple and the coming of the Messiah.

Zechariah received eight visions from the Lord in a single night, all relating to the rebuilding and restoration of Jerusalem or the coming of the Messiah. Some of these picture the coming Messiah as a humble servant. One of the more vivid proclaims: "See, your king comes to you, righteous and having salvation, gentle and riding on a donkey, on a colt, the foal of a donkey" (9:9). This is one of three hundred prophecies specifically fulfilled by Jesus Christ.

Zechariah also tells of the Messiah coming in glory. Chapters 12–14 speak of a time when the people of Jerusalem will see the Lord coming. Zechariah says, "They will look on me, the one they have pierced" (12:10). This coming is climaxed in chapter 14 when the prophet writes, "On that day his feet [the Lord's] will stand on the Mount of Olives, east of Jerusalem, and the Mount of Olives will be split in two from east to west" (14:4). He goes on to reveal, "The Lord will be king over the whole earth. On that day there will be one Lord, and his name the only name" (14:9).

It was from this same Mount of Olives that Jesus ascended in plain sight of his disciples. At this very spot the angels declared, "This same Jesus, who has been taken from you into heaven, will come back in the same way you have seen him go into heaven" (Acts 1:11).

MALACHI

The final book of the Minor Prophets is also the final book of the Old Testament in the Protestant Bible. Malachi, who wrote around 400 B.C., was followed by a four-hundred-year period called "the silent years." The next prophetic voice to be heard in Israel would be the one "crying in the wilderness" of Judea (Mark 1:3, NASB). His name was John the Baptist.

In what should have been a time of great joy with the restoration now complete, Malachi was sent to confront the returned and settled exiles. Things had already started to slip. God was not pleased.

The first issue Malachi confronted was the kind of offerings the people were bringing to the rebuilt temple. God had asked for unblemished sacrifices. He wanted his people's best as an expression of their trust in his provision and as an act of gratitude for all he had done. Instead, the people were bringing the "leftovers" of their flocks. God sent two messages through Malachi: (1) I am not pleased, and (2) I will not accept your offering (1:10). Instead of finding delight in bringing offerings to God, the people considered it a burden.

The second problem Malachi confronted was the unfaithfulness of the priests of Israel. Unlike Levi, the father of their tribe and a man in whom nothing false could be found and one who gave true instruction, the priests of the returned remnant were leading people astray. God was not pleased.

The third issue Malachi confronted was that of divorce. The men of Israel were divorcing their wives and marrying foreign women. God let the nation know how he felt: "I hate divorce" (2:16).

Finally, Malachi addressed the people's failure to honor God by giving the required tithe to the work of the temple. God issued a scathing indictment of this offense as robbing God (3:8). Then he made a promise. If the people of Israel would bring the full tithe into the storehouse of the Temple, God promised to throw open the floodgates of heaven and pour out his blessing (3:10).

The book appropriately ends with a message of the coming of the Day of the Lord, the event Israel had looked forward to for most of its history. The Day of the Lord is the climactic period of human history when God will assume his rightful place in relationship to the world. The wicked will be judged and the righteous will be rewarded. Things will be as they were intended to be.

Malachi closes with a promise that the prophet Elijah, one of two Old Testament characters taken from the planet before they died, would come and prepare the way for that great day. The Old Testament comes to a close. The New will open with the fulfillment of Malachi's promise — the coming of John the Baptist.

Enjoying the Bible: Studying the Word

"Study to show thyself approved," wrote the apostle Paul (2 Timothy 2:15, KJV). To really enjoy the Bible, it is necessary to become a student of the Bible. When we study, we dig in and begin to discover the depth and richness of this marvelous book from God.

Early in my spiritual journey I found myself wanting to know more than I could learn by simply reading or hearing the Bible. I found myself asking all kinds of questions: "What does that word really mean?" "What caused Paul to write that?" "Where in the world did the Colossians live anyway?"

My questions motivated me to begin to study the Bible. This discipline changed my life so completely that I ended up going into the ministry and devoting my life to the study and teaching of the Bible.

One of my favorite verses, and one that God used to lead me into a teaching ministry, is found in the book of Ezra. When Ezra first came to Israel in around 457 B.C., at the time of Israel's restoration from the Babylonian captivity, he was described in this manner: "For Ezra had devoted himself to the study and observance of the Law of the Lord, and to teaching its decrees and laws in Israel" (Ezra 7:10).

I was one of those lucky guys (I think?) who was always able to get by in school without much study. I actually didn't like to study and did as little of it as possible. It wasn't until I became interested in the Bible that I began to really study. Studying the Bible is different from studying any other subject. It carries with it a special blessing that you won't experience when studying the French Revolution or advanced calculus. Studying the Bible is fun, rewarding, and life-changing! How should you start this discipline?

Have you ever observed how hard it is to do some jobs without the proper tools? I've spent hours trying to fix my motorcycle only to give up and take it to a mechanic who fixes the problem in about thirty seconds. What is the difference? Usually, I don't have the right tool and he does. Studying the Bible requires a few good tools. I am often asked, "How did you get so much out of that passage?" My answer is usually, "I used my tools." I'm going to suggest a few good tools for you to acquire and then show you a few simple ways to study. In the next chapter I'll go into a more detailed approach to study.

The first tool you need is, once again, a good Bible. If you are reading a paraphrase or older translation, pick up a good newer translation like the New International version or the New American Standard Bible to use as your study Bible. When you study, you want to make sure you have an accurate text to begin with. Many of the other tools are geared to the language of the text.

The second tool I would recommend is a pen and pad of paper. You will be amazed how much you can learn with just these tools.

One of the most effective ways of learning more about a text is to carefully observe it and take notes on what you discover.

I am a logical and linear thinker. Because of this, I have learned much about the Bible by simply outlining passages. Let me walk you through a simple way to outline a passage:

1. ***You begin by picking a passage you want to study.*** Let's say you choose Philippians 3:1-11. You would begin by writing this text on the top of your pad.
2. ***Next, you read the text and attempt to discover its main point.*** In this case, you might decide the passage is about Paul's value system. You would write this under the text reference.
3. ***Then you go back and read the passage a third time, attempting to see how Paul explains his value system in these verses.*** As you read, you see three main transitions in the pas- sage. These transitions are going to be the main points in my outline. You observe that Paul begins by talking about his old value system. Then he stops and assesses that old system as compared to his relationship with Jesus. Finally, he tells us what is really important to him now.

After these three steps, your outline looks like this:

Philippians 3:1-11

"Paul's Value system"

I.   Paul's Old Values (verses 1-6)
II. Paul's Assessment of His Old Values (verses 7-9)
III. Paul's New Values (verses 10-11)

At this point, let me make an observation. It would be my guess that if you were to do no more than this, you would have become more of a student of the Bible than 90 percent of the men and women who have ever opened the book. If I were to ask you the main point of Philippians 3, you could immediately tell me, "That is a text in which Paul tells us a bit about his value system." How many of your church friends would have the ability to tell you such a thing? Not many, I bet!

Let's continue. Remember, so far all you are using is a Bible, pen, and pad of paper. Actually, you also are using the most important tool in Bible study — your mind.

4. *You take your outline and add some meat to it.* Under point I, what does Paul tell us about his old value system? Read verses 1–6 again. He issues a warning and then describes seven characteristics of his previous way of life. You add these to your outline and now it looks like this:

I. Paul's Old Values (verses 1-6)
  b. Paul's warning (verses 1-3)
  c. Paul's credentials (verses 4-6)
    1. Circumcised on the eighth day
    2. Nation of Israel
    3. Tribe of Benjamin
    4. Hebrew of Hebrews
    5. Pharisee
    6. Persecutor
    7. Legalistic perfection

Let's skip down to the third main point in our outline. What are Paul's new values? He names six. Let's add these to your outline:

III. Paul's New Values (verses 10-11)
   a. Gain Christ
   b. Know Christ
   c. Experience the power of His resurrection
   d. Share the fellowship of His sufferings
   e. Be like Him in death
   f. Attain resurrection from dead

At this point you have a simple outline of this passage. Now you can do one of two things. You might take some time to compare the lists. You also might reflect on the intensity of Paul's evaluation of these two sets of values. If you want to go further, you can use more tools.

One of the simplest tools available is a study Bible. Many good ones are available. I sometimes use a *New International Study Bible*. Some of my friends prefer the *Ryrie Study Bible*. In my study Bible I can turn to the book of Philippians and access a great deal of study material.

For example, a study Bible usually provides a brief synopsis of each book and its historical background. In the notes on Philippians, you would discover that Paul is writing the book while imprisoned in Rome. He is about to appear before the emperor. His life is at stake. Suddenly, Paul's value system takes on new meaning. It is as if you are reading a guide to what is really important when you are facing death.

Turning to any page with actual Bible text on it, you will notice that the bottom of the page is filled with notes corresponding to the numbers of certain verses. These notes might explain the significance of the seven credentials Paul uses to describe his old value system. For instance, to be circumcised on the eighth day tells you that Paul was a Jew from birth, not a convert to Judaism.

To be from the tribe of Benjamin identifies him as a Jewish "blue blood" from one of the tribes that did not defect during the period of the Divided kingdom. To be a Pharisee means that Paul was a religious and civil leader of the Jews with great authority and prestige.

Every phrase paints a bit more of a picture of a man who had it made by the standards of the society in which he lived. Paul had it made — and lost it all. And yet, his loss for the sake of Christ became the source of his new values. He even says that it was all just *skubala*. We'll look at the significance of this word in the next chapter when we explore advanced study techniques.

A good study Bible also provides margin references to other verses dealing with the same subject. By looking up these references, more light is shed on your passage.

Finally, many study Bibles are filled with additional information in the back. My *Thompson Chain Reference Bible* has an entire section on biblical archaeology that would take years to totally digest. It also contains detailed maps of Paul's missionary travels, showing where the Philippians lived and how they fit geographically with the rest of the ancient world. This Bible also has a topical index where I can find every reference in the Bible to values, among other subjects. One good tool goes a long way.

At this point, we are barely scratching the surface of Bible study!

CHAPTER 4
The Gospels

§

The Bible is the cradle wherein Christ is laid.

— MARTIN LUTHER

THE NEW TESTAMENT

THE FOURTH MAJOR DIVISION OF the Bible begins what we have come to know as the New Testament. This title derives from two sources. The first is the historical reality that the emphasis now moves beyond a limited focus on Israel to a new, broader message concerning God's plans and purposes for all humanity through Jesus Christ. The second is the reality that through Jesus the New Covenant between God and humanity promised by the prophet Jeremiah has been inaugurated.

For our purposes I am going to divide the New Testament into four logical sections. In this chapter we will attempt to understand and enjoy the historical narratives of the four gospels. In chapter 5 we will explore the life of the early church recorded in the book of Acts. In chapter 6 we'll cover the teaching letters of the early church, the Epistles. Finally, chapter 7 will provide a brief synopsis of the apocalyptic visions of the future found in the book of Revelation.

Understanding the Gospels

The New Testament begins with four books we refer to as the Gospels, or the historical record of the life and teaching of Jesus Christ. Technically, there is only one gospel, written from four different viewpoints. In the earliest manuscripts available, these documents are simply entitled "According to . . . " with each writer's name attached to his particular work. As with the Old Testament, no original manuscripts exist.

The "according to" title is very appropriate. It is as if the subject matter is so extraordinary and overwhelming that it requires a number of people to capture the "big picture." I often think of it using the analogy of four blind men attempting to describe an elephant.

One is touching the trunk and announces, "An elephant is an animal with a long trunk proceeding from its head with which it breathes and feeds itself." Another of the men is holding its tail and reports, "An elephant is an animal with a short tail, devoid of any body hair." The third runs his hands along the side of the elephant and writes, "Elephants are huge mammals with massive girth, and rough hides." Finally, the fourth is holding an ear. He tells us, "An elephant is a beast with large, floppy ears that hang at the side of its head." When we put the reports of all four together, we begin to understand what an elephant looks like.

Sometimes I also imagine the four accounts of Jesus' life like a surround-sound stereo system. One account of the story is the center speaker, with two others functioning as front and rear speakers to enhance the sound. Finally, a fourth speaker called a sub-woofer enhances the bass line.

The listener sits in the middle and enjoys the fullness such a system delivers. The sound is fuller and more complete than any monophonic or stereo reproduction of the music could ever give. I guess you could say that God has given us a surround-sound gospel.

MARK

If I were asked to reconfigure the layout of the New Testament I would start with Mark's gospel. I will address it first because of the unique role it plays in the scholarly assessment of how the four gospel documents originated.

Mark is the earliest of what are known as the three synoptic gospels. The word *synoptic* means "to see together." If you are a new student of the Bible and you begin by reading the New Testament in order, you will start to wonder why so much of the content of the first three books is so similar. You will read the same story a number of times and say to your-self, *I think I just read this in Matthew!* You would be correct.

Many biblical scholars believe that the synoptics (Matthew, Mark, and Luke) shared a common source document, usually referred to as Q, from which the authors wrote their accounts of Jesus' life. This academic hypothesis (which cannot be proven at the current time because no earlier source has actually been found) is based on the fact that the first three gospels do share much in common. Over 90 percent of the content of Mark can be found in either Matthew or Luke. In contrast, over 90 percent of John is totally unique to his gospel. Written much later than the first three, it was as if John were making sure that the events he recorded were preserved for posterity.

There are four possibilities regarding the Q theory. The first is that no such source ever existed and the hypothesis is simply wrong. In this case, the eyewitness testimony of these authors is similar merely because they all were there and wrote about the same events.

The second possibility is that these documents were simply transcriptions of the oral tradition that had been circulating for years before being written down. As mentioned in an earlier chapter, oral tradition was the primary way of preserving history in the ancient world, was extremely effective, and was often trusted as more accurate than written documents.

The third possibility is that a Q source did exist and has been lost. Perhaps someday archaeologists will discover such a source. Because the earliest of the four gospels was not put in writing until ten to twenty years after the life of Jesus, it would not be impossible that such a written document or a collection of written documents existed. The primary argument against such a possibility is that with the massive manuscript evidence we do have, one would think that at least some fragment of Q would have survived.

The fourth possibility is that Mark is Q. This is a relatively common theory held by many biblical scholars. For this reason I would place Mark at the beginning of the New Testament documents. We know that it is the earliest of the four gospels, written probably in the early '40s or '50s of the first century. The author, Mark, has historically been identified as the John Mark of the book of Acts.

Although he started his career with Paul, he ended it with Peter. The historical consensus is that Mark is actually the gospel "according to" Peter, written down by Mark. It is the connection of this gospel with Peter that gave this account its credibility and authority in the early church.

Mark is the only document of the four that identifies itself as a "gospel." Mark begins by informing us that this is "The beginning of the gospel about Jesus Christ." The book of Mark, like each of the gospels, has distinguishing characteristics.

For one, it is brief and to the point, the shortest of the four gospels. It reflects the no-nonsense approach you might expect were Peter telling the story. Each of the four gospels seems to be written to a specific audience, and it has been suggested that Mark's audience was Roman. The fast-paced action and lack of extraneous detail seem to support this theory. The most repeated word in Mark's gospel is *immediately.* He treats events with a single sentence that might occupy many paragraphs in Matthew or Luke.

Because Mark is the earliest of the gospel accounts — and the most likely to be a type of Q source — I will use it as the basis for describing the primary content of all four gospel narratives. Each contains material on the following periods of Jesus' life and ministry.

Period One: The Early Ministry of Jesus. When we think of the life of Christ, most of us logically begin with his birth and the events surrounding Christmas. Mark jumps right into his account with the role of John the Baptist and Jesus' baptism by John. As is the case in the other two synoptics, this event is followed by Christ's temptation in the wilderness.

From there Mark moves rapidly into a narrative of the ministry of Jesus. We see him healing the sick, casting demons out of the possessed, and proclaiming the message of the kingdom of God.

As you read Mark and the other gospels, it is helpful to track the movements of Jesus. His ministry can be divided into several periods based upon which part of Israel he was located. There are at least five periods of Jesus' ministry when divided this way:

1. The Early Judean Period (only recorded in John's gospel)
2. The Great Galilean Period (all four record parts of this period)
3. The Period Beyond the Jordan (primarily in Luke)
4. The Later Judean Period (parts in all four gospels)
5. The Final Week in Jerusalem (all four)

Tracking Christ's travels also can be a helpful tool in getting a handle on his ministry. Notice how a careful reading of Mark requires a good understanding of the geography of Israel:

1. Jesus' baptism in Judea (1:9)
2. Off to Capernaum in Galilee (1:21)
3. On the far side of the Sea of Galilee (5:1)
4. In Jesus' hometown of Nazareth (6:1)
5. In the region of Tyre and Sidon (7:24)
6. Back to Bethsaida (8:22)
7. Off to Caesarea Philippi (8:27)
8. Back to Capernaum (9:33)
9. Into the region across the Jordan (10:1)

By the middle of the tenth chapter, Jesus is heading toward Jerusalem and the events of the final week of his life. Chapters 11–16 all take place in and around Jerusalem.

Period Two: The Middle Ministry. Mark's middle chapters contain highlights of the primary ministry of Jesus. Much of this period takes place in Galilee, his home base. Along with healing and casting out demons, we see Jesus performing miracles and teaching.

Much of the action of these middle chapters involves the relationship of Jesus with his disciples. Training the Twelve was at the heart of all he did during this period.

Much of Jesus' teaching at this time was done in parables. A parable is a simple story that illustrates a profound truth and often involves the use of nature or other familiar items to make its point. Mark records many of the parables that Luke and Matthew also have preserved, such as the parable of the sower and the parable of the mustard seed.

All three of the synoptics record the miracles of feeding the four thousand and the five thousand, walking on water, and calming the waves on the Sea of Galilee.

Period Three: The Final Week. All four of the gospels record the events of the final week of Jesus' earthly life and ministry. This was the week when Jesus entered the city of Jerusalem on what we call Palm Sunday and was greeted by crowds cheering "Hosanna!" It was the week when his conflict with Israel's religious establishment reached its peak. It was the week when he gathered with his disciples in the Upper Room and instituted the celebration of the New Covenant.

This final week reached its climax with the trials of Jesus. Now the crowds' cries became "Crucify him!" All four gospel accounts describe Christ's crucifixion ad his death on the cross. All four gospels end with the record of Jesus' resurrection and his post-resurrection appearances to the disciples.

THE UNIQUENESS OF MATTHEW
Each gospel account has unique characteristics and material. Although the book of Matthew contains much of the same material

as Mark and Luke, Matthew organizes this material in a different manner and with a different emphasis.

The book of Matthew appears to be written to a primarily Jewish audience. Matthew himself was a Jew and one of the original twelve disciples. Also known as Levi, Matthew was a tax collector who became a follower of Jesus.

Matthew, along with Luke, begins his gospel earlier in the life of Jesus than Mark. Matthew and Luke both contain portions of what we think of as the Christmas story. They also both focus on Jesus' Jewish heritage by including his genealogy in their accounts. Matthew is careful to point out how many details surrounding Christ's birth fulfilled Old Testament prophecies of the coming Messiah. One of his most common phrases is, "This happened to fulfill what was said." Matthew's gospel is organized in a very systematic manner, grouping large amounts of material from the life of Christ in topical fashion. For instance, in chapter 13 Matthew records seven of Jesus' parables concerning the kingdom of God. In chapters 5–7 the Sermon on the Mount receives its most comprehensive treatment in any of the gospels. Some scholars argue that this material was not originally delivered in one sitting. This is merely scholarly speculation, but it would be consistent with how Matthew organized his gospel.

THE UNIQUENESS OF LUKE

Luke was a traveling companion of the apostle Paul and not one of the original disciples. Like Mark's gospel and Mark's relationship with Peter, it is Luke's relationship with Paul that gave this account its place of authority in the early church.

Luke was a doctor and wrote with an academic sense of precision. Note how in the opening statements of the gospel Luke explains that he desires to take the various accounts of Christ's life and organize them in a more efficient and complete manner.

Matthew seems to organize his book around themes or topics. Luke organizes his chronologically. His style has suggested to scholars that in the same way Matthew targeted a Jewish audience of his peers, Luke's gospel is tailor-made for a Greek-speaking and Greek-thinking audience. This would make sense, because Paul was uniquely called to be the apostle to the non-Jewish world.

While Matthew covers the Sermon on the Mount, Luke records what has been called the Sermon on the Plain (chapter 6). Luke's unique material also includes a series of pas- sages, which occurs during the Later Judean Ministry and the Perean Ministry. This was during a three-month-or-so period that immediately preceded Christ's entry into Jerusalem for the Passion Week.

It was during this time that Jesus told the parable of the prodigal son (15:11-32), the parable of the rich man and Lazarus (16:19-31), and the parable of the Pharisee and the tax collector (18:9-14).

This period ends as Jesus hears of the death of his friend Lazarus and heads to Bethany for one of the greatest miracles of his ministry. This event logically moves us into the gospel of John because John is the only writer who records the resurrection of Lazarus from the dead.

The Uniqueness of John

As mentioned previously, the most distinct book of the four gospels is that written by the Apostle John. John also is unique in the place he chooses to begin his narrative. Mark starts with Jesus' public ministry. Matthew and Luke take us back to his birth. John carries his audience all the way back into eternity, to the beginning of time itself: "In the beginning was the Word" (1:1). Echoing the opening words of Genesis, John speaks of Jesus as the Word, or the *Logos*.

John's gospel is usually dated quite late. It was in all probability written between 85 and 90 A.D. By this time, John was working in the region of Asia Minor as the leader of the church in Ephesus, one of the intellectual centers of the ancient world. Asia Minor was a land bridge between East and West, a melting pot of the peoples and ideas of the first century. When John calls Jesus *Logos* he is using a Greek philosophical concept debated for centuries. As the Greeks viewed it, *Logos* was the source of order, meaning, and purpose in the universe.

John opens his work by declaring that there is in fact a *Logos*, the source of all that exists. At this point, a first- century Greek audience would still be shaking their heads in affirmation. Then John drops the bomb: "The *Logos* became flesh and pitched his tent among us" (1:14, my paraphrase). John declares that the source of order, meaning, and purpose in the universe is not an impersonal concept as the Greeks imagined, but a person! Jesus Christ was and is the *Logos!*

John's is the only gospel that records what is called the Early Judean Ministry of Jesus. This was the time when Christ first cleansed the temple in Jerusalem by chasing out the moneychangers (chapter 2). It was when Jesus went to the wedding in Cana and turned water into wine (also chapter 2).

It also was in this early ministry that Jesus met a Pharisee named Nicodemus at night (chapter 3). During this encounter Jesus taught Nicodemus that all men and women must experience a spiritual birth if they are to enter the kingdom of God. Only John records the words of Jesus, "You must be born again" (3:7).

Another distinctive of the gospel of John is its emphasis on the concept of life. The word *life* appears so frequently that John has at times been called the Gospel of Life. From the very beginning John declares of Jesus, "In him was life" (1:4). It is almost impossible to understand John without knowing something about the two Greek words that we translate as "life."

The most common word for life in the Greek language is *psuche.* This was a word that spoke of normal physical existence, the kind of life that all organic entities share. This is *not* the word that occurs repeatedly throughout the gospel of John.

The second Greek word for life is *zoe.* This word speaks of a special kind of life. It is most frequently used in the Greek language to describe the uncreated life that exists *in* God and is given *by* God. This is the word repeatedly used in this Gospel.

One of Jesus' great statements that illustrates the difference between the two words is found in John 10. In this passage he talks about the difference between a good shepherd and a thief, using the terms metaphorically to speak of himself as the Good Shepherd. Jesus declares, "I have come that they may have life" (10:10).

Jesus goes on to say, "The good shepherd lays down his life for the sheep" (10:11). When you and I read these verses in an English translation we see no difference in the word *life* from one verse to the next. However, in the Greek text, two different words appear. verse 10 uses the word *zoe.* "I have come that they may have *spiritual* life." verse 11 uses the word *psuche.* "The good shepherd lays down his *physical* life for the sheep." Jesus is telling his audience that by giving his physical life in death he would make it possible to impart to them the spiritual life that only God can give. John is the Gospel of Life — *zoe.*

One final distinctive of John is his emphasis on the final week of Jesus' life and ministry. Almost half of John's gospel is written about the events of this period. There are twenty- one chapters in the book and the record of the final week begins in chapter 12. John writes the most detailed account of the evening Jesus spent with the disciples in the Upper Room, devoting nearly five chapters to it. This section of John is often called the Upper Room Discourse.

The theory behind John's gospel is that by the end of the first century the other three accounts were already in circulation. John had access to these documents and probably realized that in choosing what to include in their accounts, Mark, Matthew, and Luke had left out certain events and words that John desired to make known. His gospel became a supplementary account. It was as if Mark, Matthew, and Luke had written of three sides of the elephant and John said, "Wait a minute. You haven't told them about this long trunk that hangs down in front!" Hundreds of millions of men and women throughout the centuries have been enriched and blessed by the great picture of Jesus given by John.

ENJOYING THE BIBLE:
ADVANCED STUDY OF THE WORD

In chapter 3 I began to teach you about ways to study the Bible. I'll continue the process in this chapter by moving you to a more advanced stage of Bible study and sharing some of my favorite ways of really digging into a passage to get the most out of it.

In the last chapter I provided tips on finding a good study Bible. Now it's time to build your library with other helpful tools. You will use these books and resources again and again over the years. They are good investments. For the serious student of the Bible they will become good friends.

STUDYING HISTORICAL BACKGROUND

One of the first areas of study I undertake when working through a book of the Bible is to attempt to understand its historical background. I find this information in a number of places.

The easiest way to understand the background of a book is to use your study Bible, which typically gives a brief historical sketch at the beginning of each book. This information will start you on your quest for historical information. But where do you go from there?

One of your first acquisitions should be a good Bible dictionary. In it you will find not only a more detailed historical picture by simply looking up the title of each book, but also more in-depth historical detail by looking up various words or concepts in the text that you might not understand. For instance, let's say you are studying the book of John. Opening your dictionary to "John," you would find listings for all the major biblical characters named John.

Under something like "John, the Apostle" (rather than, for instance, "John, the Baptist") you would be given a brief biographical sketch of the author of the book. Under "John, the Gospel" you would find the historical background you are looking for.

Consider another example. The first time John mentions the word *Pharisee*, you might find yourself wondering, *What is a Pharisee?* You pick up your Bible dictionary and look it up. This entry will tell you who the Pharisees were, the origin of their name, how they developed, and the role they played in the life of Christ and the early church.

Many excellent Bible dictionaries are available at your Christian bookstore or on the Internet. Some are actually keyed to the specific version of the Bible you use. Look through several and pick one that seems the most helpful and user-friendly to you. In this age of computers, you can get computer versions of many of these tools and some programs that contain multiple tools.

Although the information you find in a Bible dictionary is a good starting place, I usually want more information than I can get in this limited source. The next tool I would encourage you to obtain is a good Bible encyclopedia. These are usually multiple-volume works that expand the information found in a one-volume Bible dictionary. You might ask for this as a Christmas or birthday present!

A good Bible dictionary will probably have a number of paragraphs on your subject. A good Bible encyclopedia will probably have several pages! You will find an extensive section concerning the historical background of the book you are studying.

When you own a Bible dictionary and encyclopedia, you are better equipped to study the Bible than about 95 percent of the Christian world. If you want to move to the 99th percentile, you need to enter the ranks of the pros — those who make a living studying and teaching the Bible — by investing in commentaries.

Commentaries are the published works of biblical scholars on individual books of the Bible. If you are studying Philippians, for instance, you would acquire a single-volume commentary on this book. Many commentaries have now been gathered into multi-volume series. If you look at an entire series, you will notice that the series probably has a single editor, but each individual volume has its own author.

An exception to this trend in the historical background category is the *Daily Bible Study Series* by William Barclay, probably the single best source of biblical historical background material available. These volumes are a compilation of Barclay's daily column that appeared in newspapers across England in the 1940s and 1950s. If you have the ability to acquire this set, you will be set!

STUDYING BIBLICAL WORDS

In my own approach to Bible study, I follow my historical background research by doing the exercises I discussed in the preceding chapter. Once I understand the book's back- ground, I read the text to get the "big idea." Then I look at individual divisions of the book to see how this big idea is developed. I approach the text as if I am an investigative reporter attempting to put all the pieces together that explain what the author — both human and divine — was attempting to communicate. It is this detective work that leads me to the next level of study.

God speaks. That is one unique distinctive of a biblical faith. We believe that the Bible is the Word of God. The Word is made up of words. It is extremely important, then, that we understand what those words mean.

Remember, the Bible was not originally written in English. The Old Testament was written in Hebrew and the New Testament in Greek. These were the predominant languages of the people who wrote the books and of the audiences to whom the books were written. Our Bibles are translations from these original languages.

Through the years I have become convinced that the men and women who have translated the Bible have done a great job. These were people who loved the Bible and used their skills and gifts to attempt to bring the meaning of the original text into the language of the modern culture. Rarely do I find a passage where I substantially disagree with how the translators have handled it.

When this happens, I might be the one who still does not get the original thrust of the message.

Again, think through the picture. Jesus spoke Aramaic, the language of the Jewish people in first-century Palestine. By his time, the majority of Jews in the world spoke either Aramaic or Greek. Alexander the Great had conquered most of the Western world in the fourth century B.C., during what is called the Intertestamental Period because it sits between the end of the Old Testament era and the beginning of the New. In that time period, the Greek language spread throughout the world.

By 250 B.C. many Jews could not read the Old Testament in its original Hebrew. This dilemma led a group of Jewish scholars to gather in Alexandria, Egypt. Alexandria was a major intellectual center named after — who else? — Alexander the Great. The legend goes that seventy scholars worked for seventy days and translated the entire Old Testament from Hebrew into Greek. It was appropriately called the Septuagint, from the Greek for "seventy."

This was an extremely important work for a number of reasons. First, it shows us that the Old Testament as we know it was a recognized body of documents by 250 B.C.. Second, it enabled and still enables us to see what Old Testament scholars considered Hebrew words to mean in Greek. Their translations into Greek give us insight even today when we attempt to capture the meaning of certain Hebrew words. Finally, it set a historical precedent of translation into the vernacular to make the Bible accessible to the common man. Modern translators of the Old Testament have both Hebrew and Greek texts of the Old Testament to work from when they attempt to translate as accurately as possible into English or some other modern language.

The New Testament was written in Greek. This means that the gospel writers had to translate the teachings of Jesus from Aramaic into Greek. Because Greek was the common language of the rest of the Roman world, the letters of the rest of the New Testament were simply written in Greek to begin with. Some scholars have suggested that the book of Hebrews might have originally been written in Hebrew and then translated into Greek, but that theory is not widely held.

The point of all this discussion about translation is that we need to recognize that our Bibles contain the best efforts of biblical scholars to translate from one language to another. They are working with words. When we study the Bible, at times we will want to go back to the original words and see what they meant in historical context. We will want to become our own translators. This takes tools.

One of my earliest acquisitions was a *Vine's Expository Dictionary of New Testament Words*. This is more like a regular dictionary in the fact that it is comprised of words found in the New Testament with their original Greek words defined and explained. For instance, when reading about love in 1 Corinthians 13, I might want to know what the word *love* means in the original language. Actually, I might be confused because my translation says "love" and a friend's reads "charity."

In *Vine's* I discover there are several Greek words in the original language translated into the English word *love*. Fortunately, *Vine's* lists the main texts where each of these words is used, then gives the Greek word that has been translated and its definition. Thus I find in the Corinthians passage that the Greek word *agape* appears every time my Bible says "love."

By reading the *Vine's* definition of *agape*, I gain a deeper understanding of what Paul was talking about. And by reading the definitions of the words Paul did not use, I also learn any subtle nuance the word *agape* contains that the others do not.

Word studies are a great way to add depth to your understanding of the Bible. But good word studies go beyond exploring the simple definition of a word. Sometimes they involve knowing a bit of grammar. This will require more tools.

As with historical study, there is a logical progression in word and grammatical study tools. From a one-volume word study book like *Vine's* you can move to *The New International Dictionary of New Testament Theology*, a three-volume set edited by Colin Brown, each of which is hearty enough to hold down the corner of a tent in a hurricane! Whereas *Vine's* provides a one- or two-paragraph definition of *love*, this comprehensive set offers ten or twelve pages of information on this single word!

From this kind of resource you can move in several directions. One is to go to analytical lexicons and find the exact grammatical form of a word and its various grammatical components. (Without some background in Hebrew and Greek, this can be quite a challenge!) To do this kind of study you will either need to know Greek or need to acquire an interlinear Bible containing the Greek and Hebrew text with the English translation located immediately under the original language. This will help you identify the exact form of the word to look up in the lexicon. Then the lexicon will give you a string of information such as "1 per., sing., fut." Thus you learn the word is a verb used in the first person, singular, and future tense. In this case, *love* is translated "I will love." If the lexicon says the word is "3 pers., pl., aor." you know to translate the word *agape* as "we have loved."

If I have just lost you, hold on for a moment. I will get back to a more basic approach. If I have just thrilled you, you might need to think about taking some seminary classes!

An easier approach to grammatical study is to use a good commentary. To get into this kind of material you'll probably need to find a scholarly work and not just a popular commentary. Such a commentary will take you to a verse and tell you something like, "*Love* here is the word *agape*. It appears in the first person, singular number, and future tense. As such it should be translated 'I will love.'" In other words, the commentary has done the work for you.

You might be thinking, *Why not just buy the commentary?* The problem is that often the commentator didn't choose to detail the word or phrase you want information concerning. Then you have to do it the hard way.

A note of caution here: I always go to a commentary last. It is a quick way to understand a passage, but not always the best. I find something important about the very process of study. I like to do all my own work before I see what some- one else has discovered. Sometimes I actually discover that I disagree with the commentator. At other times I discover something of the commentator's prejudices concerning a specific text. It all makes Bible study an exciting adventure.

When you study a passage in its historical, grammatical, and biblical context, you have done most of the work serious Bible students tackle when attempting to gain deeper understanding of God's Word. I believe you will really enjoy this discipline and find it tremendously helpful in the adventure of mastering the Word.

CHAPTER 5

The Book of Acts

§

Understanding Acts

THE FIFTH DIVISION OF OUR study is composed of a single document. Called "Acts" in our English Bibles, in most Greek texts it is entitled "The Acts of the Apostles". Serving as a transition between the Gospels and their record of the life of Jesus and the Epistles containing instructions to the apostolic churches, the book is so significant we will devote an entire chapter to it.

Acts is about the life of the early church and was written around 60 A.D. by Luke, the physician. As we saw in the last chapter, Luke was the traveling companion of the apostle Paul and wrote the gospel that bears his name. Both the gospel of Luke and the book of Acts were placed within the New Testament canon on the basis of Paul's relationship to these documents. Apostolic authorship was one of the measures of whether a document was considered authoritative in the life of the church.

Because Acts explains why Paul ended up in Rome, some scholars believe it was originally written o serve as part of Paul's defense before the Roman emperor. Luke definitely paints a positive picture of the Roman Empire at this point in history and shows Paul's role as a Roman citizen who has appealed his cause to Caesar.

PART ONE: CHAPTERS 1-7

Although a careful reading of Acts leads one to conclude that Paul is the primary character, the first twelve chapters actually describe life in the early church before Paul took center stage. The primary character at this point is Peter, and the focal group is the church in and around Jerusalem. We often forget that for the first years following Jesus' resurrection the church was made up almost exclusively of Jewish converts.

Acts begins at the Mount of Olives where Jesus, surrounded by His disciples, promises the gift of the Holy Spirit and commissions them to be his witnesses to the entire world. His last words before ascending into heaven were, "You will receive power when the Holy Spirit comes on you; and you will be my witnesses in Jerusalem, and in all Judea and Samaria, and to the ends of the earth" (1:8).

This mandate forms a simple outline of the entire book of Acts. Chapters 1–8 portray how the disciples were witnesses in Jerusalem. Chapters 9–12 depict the spread of the message outside Jerusalem into Judea and Samaria. Chapters 13–28 describe how the gospel left the narrow confines of the Jewish world and spread to the Gentile cultures from Antioch in Syria all the way to Rome.

THE ASCENSION

The early chapters of Acts contain several critical events in the life of early Christianity. Chapter 1 features the eyewitness account of an event that occurred roughly forty days after Jesus Christ was crucified, buried, and rose from the dead. Jesus had repeatedly told his followers that the day was coming when he would return to his Father in the exalted position he had occupied from all eternity.

In clear view of approximately 120 men and women, Jesus physically ascended into the air and disappeared from their sight. The text leaves no question that the gathered group of observers was stunned and confused, so much so that angelic messengers were sent to explain what these was returning to the Father, and one day he would return in exactly the same manner and, as many believe, to exactly the same place!

PENTECOST

Chapter 2 describes what happened ten days later as the Jews were celebrating the Feast of Pentecost (or Weeks). The festival, always fifty days after Passover, was a time of both thanksgiving and expectation as the people remembered how God provided for their needs when they traveled from Egypt to Canaan during the exodus and how he would provide for them again in the coming fall harvest.

During this celebration, the group of 120 disciples gathered in an upper room. While together, a mighty wind began to blow and what appeared to be tongues of fire came and rested on them. Suddenly, these men and women began to speak in foreign languages they had never learned. Because Pentecost was one of the three major festivals of the Jewish year, Jerusalem was filled with people from all over the ancient world, many of whom flocked to hear the disciples declaring spiritual truth in their own languages.

We are told that the presence of this crowd of observers prompted Peter to stand in their midst and preach his first sermon since Jesus had risen from the dead. He told the crowd that they were witnessing the fulfillment of Old Testament prophecy, reminding them of Joel's promise that God would "pour out" his

Spirit and "your sons and your daughters will prophesy" (Joel 2:28). This supernatural phenomenon was the proof that the risen Christ had resumed his place in the Father's presence. Peter boldly proclaimed this Jesus they crucified, but whom God raised from the dead (Acts 2:23-24). Three thousand people believed and the New Testament church was born.

From this point forward in the book of Acts, the Holy Spirit plays a central role. Some have even suggested that the title of the book should be "The Acts of the Holy Spirit Through the Apostles". It is a transformed band of men and women who march into Jerusalem with boldness and conviction and declare that Jesus is the risen Messiah.

These chapters of Acts also provide a bird's-eye view of daily life in the early church. Those who believed met together daily in the temple courts to hear from the apostles. They also met in individual homes and shared meals while devoting themselves to prayer, study of the apostles' teaching, and fellowship. The dynamism of this Spirit-empowered group was so contagious that new believers were joining the Jesus movement every day.

A new and radical kind of caring characterized these men and women. With a transformed understanding of life and reality, they moved away from self-centered accumulation of goods and possessions and began to share all they had with one another so that there was not a needy person in their midst (2:44-46).

And how did "the establishment" react to this "revolutionary" group? As was the case with Jesus himself, hostility and opposition quickly arose. Some Christ-followers were beaten; others were arrested and jailed. The climax of this section of Acts was the martyrdom of a young man named Stephen. The angry crowd could not bear to hear the truth he spoke, and so he was stoned as a heretic to the Jewish tradition.

PART TWO: CHAPTERS 8–12

Stephen's death serves as the transition to the second part of Acts. The next few chapters show how the first followers moved beyond the walls of Jerusalem in response to persecution. As they spread out, the gospel message began to be shared with a non-Jewish audience, a shift that leads to the third part of the book. Chapters 8–12 also introduce the main character for the remainder of Acts, a young Pharisee named Saul who gave his approval to Stephen's stoning.

THE CONVERSION OF PAUL

Following Stephen's stoning, Saul goes to the Jewish authorities and receives permission to go to Damascus to find others who are proclaiming this "heresy" about Jesus. The language is vivid when it describes Saul as "breathing out murderous threats" (9:1).

One of the Bible's most significant events takes place on the road between Jerusalem and Damascus. A blinding light knocks Saul to the ground and a voice asks, "Saul, Saul, why do you persecute me?" Saul instinctively knew God was speaking to him and follows with his own question, "Who are you, Lord?" The answer changed Saul's life and the history of Western civilization. "I am Jesus, whom you are persecuting" (9:5).

I have tried to imagine what must have gone through Saul's mind in that moment. Everything he had believed suddenly came tumbling down. The implications of his role in Stephen's death and his hatred for the followers of the new Way were wrong. His zeal was misdirected. The persecutor was about to become a proclaimer of the message of Jesus.

THE BREAKOUT

The next few chapters of Acts record the gospel's spread from one world to another. Actually, it all began in Acts 8 when Philip, like Stephen a deacon of the church, went to Samaria (the same region where Jesus encountered the woman at the well).

Under Jewish tradition, the Samaritans were "unclean" and any conversation with them was forbidden. But Philip told them about Jesus — and they believed! In response to Philip's ministry, Peter and John went to Samaria as well. As they prayed for the Samaritans, the Holy Spirit came on these new converts just as he had on the Jews at Pentecost. The journey to Samaria was a short one geographically. But culturally and sociologically, it was a million miles away. And more was to come.

Acts 10 tells the story of Peter's visit to the coastal town of Joppa. Tired and hungry, he went to a rooftop to pray while dinner was being prepared. As Peter fell into a trance, God gave him a vision of a large sheet being lowered from heaven filled with animals that were unclean according to Jewish law. A voice instructed Peter to kill and eat these animals, but Peter refused. He would have no contact with anything Jewish law declared unclean. The voice replied, "Do not call anything impure that God has made clean" (10:15).

The message from God had much broader significance than its relationship to Jewish dietary laws. God was preparing Peter for an encounter with a Roman centurion named Cornelius. Immediately following the vision, servants from Cornelius knocked at the door. They told Peter they had been sent to bring him to Caesarea, to the home of a Roman! Peter suddenly understood the real meaning of the vision. Gentiles were not "unclean." They were created by God and needed to hear about Jesus. Peter went.

The final barrier between Jew and Gentile had been broken down. The message was clear. Jesus was not just for Jews. When Jesus said to go into all the world (Matthew 28:19), he meant *all* the world: Jew, Samaritan, and Gentile. The stage was set for part 3 of Acts.

PART THREE: CHAPTERS 13–28

The final sixteen chapters of Acts record the four preaching journeys of the apostle Paul. Early in this section, Saul takes on the name Paul. Saul was a Jewish name; Paul, a Greek one. To identify with his audience and as an act of humility, the man who bore the name of Israel's first king now took a name that meant "small."

THE CALL AND JOURNEYS

Paul had come to Antioch in Syria to minister to the believers there. While in Antioch, God spoke through the gathered fellowship that Paul and his friend Barnabas should be set apart to preach the gospel. So they responded in obedience and set out for Cyprus.

The first expedition led Paul and Barnabas from Cyprus to the coast of modern Turkey. From there they headed inland to four cities: Antioch in Pisidia, Iconium, Lystra, and Derbe in southern Galatia. Everywhere they went, they spread the message about Jesus. Those who believed began to gather together in groups we call churches.

After returning from this first trip, Paul and the brothers from Antioch went to Jerusalem for what many believe was the first church council. The issue at stake was how much of first-century Judaism Gentiles needed to embrace to be saved. The outcome of the council freed Gentiles from any Jewish requirements other than social sensitivity to their Jewish brothers.

Christians today are extremely indebted to the work of the Holy Spirit in guiding these early church leaders. In the next chapter, when you read the synopsis of the book of Galatians, you will discover more of the issues decided at this important meeting.

The results of the council motivated Paul and his companions to head further west in their mission. The account of Paul's second expedition begins in Acts 16 and runs through the middle of Acts 18. On this journey, Paul received a vision that led him into Europe to travel as far as Corinth and Athens before heading back to home base in Antioch.

Beginning in Acts 18:23, we read how Paul again headed west. This time his primary destination was the city of Ephesus, where he spent more than two years teaching and preaching. From this ministry, the entire Roman province of Asia heard the good news and churches were planted across the region. This third journey ended with another trip to Jerusalem, where Paul was recognized by the Jewish religious leadership and attacked. His plea as a Roman citizen resulted in imprisonment in Caesarea and finally in Rome.

The fourth journey is the account of Paul's trip from Caesarea to Rome. By the time the book of Acts ends, we have traveled thousands of miles with this amazing man and his friends and have covered almost thirty years of early church history. The book also sets a context for what is to follow: the letters to these churches contained in the rest of the New Testament.

ENJOYING THE BIBLE:
MEMORIZING AND MEDITATING ON THE WORD

MEMORIZING GOD'S WORD

One of my favorite verses in the book of Acts contains the final words Jesus spoke to his disciples before his ascension into heaven.

In it Jesus both made a promise and gave a com- mission: "You will receive power when the Holy Spirit come son you; and you will be my witnesses in Jerusalem, and in all Judea and Samaria, and to the ends of the earth" (1:8). As I typed this verse in the manuscript, I did not go to my Bible and look it up in the first chapter of Acts. I wrote it from memory. This is one of many Bible verses I have memorized.

I am very grateful that early in my own experience of understanding and enjoying the Bible I was challenged to begin to memorize God's Word. I can remember that part of my motivation came from several verses that promise God's blessing for undertaking this enterprise. The psalmist wrote, "I have hidden your word in my heart that I might not sin against you" (Psalm 119:11). I needed all the help I could get to overcome patterns I had developed that were out of conformity with God's plan for my life. Memorizing Scripture was critical for me.

Early on I also heard someone speak on God's promise of prosperity from Joshua 1. God himself was preparing Joshua to lead the armies of Israel across the Jordan to conquer Canaan. In his final instructions to Joshua, God said, "Do not let this Book of the Law depart from your mouth; meditate on it day and night, so that you may be careful to do everything written in it. Then you will be prosperous and successful" (Joshua 1:8).

Joshua needed to do three things in order to experience God's promise of success and prosperity. The first was not to let the Book of the Law depart from his mouth. I believe this is a reference to memorizing Scripture. It is part of God's formula for success and prosperity his way. I am not a genius, but I can certainly figure out that we ought to take advantage of anything God says will guarantee prosperity and success!

Early in my spiritual journey I also heard someone speak on a text from the prophet Jeremiah. In the midst of what is predominantly a very pessimistic book, Jeremiah proclaims, "Your words were found and I ate them; and your words became for me my joy and my heart's delight, for I am called by your name, O Lord God Almighty" (Jeremiah 15:16). The idea of "eating" God's Word is found repeatedly in the Old Testament. It is an image of internalizing the Word by memorizing it.

I knew I needed all the joy and delight I could get! So I began to memorize the Bible. I still work on this spiritual discipline. I do it now for other reasons. I have become aware of how much our minds are like extremely complex computers. They tend to respond to the data we program them with. I am also aware of the battle that goes on in our inner lives between the thoughts and ideas of the fallen world system — what Paul calls the mind of the flesh — and the thoughts and promptings of the Spirit.

I want to have a transformed mind (Romans 12:1-2). I want to cultivate the mind of Christ (Philippians 2:5). Memorization is a powerful tool that the Holy Spirit uses to accomplish these purposes.

Over the years I have discovered the secret of memorization. Are you ready? It takes work! One of my close pastor friends begins his message every Sunday by quoting from memory the chapter of the Bible his message is taken from. He has memorized most of the New Testament and large passages from the Old. He puts me to shame in this discipline. Many in his congregation think he has the gift of a photographic memory. He does not. How does he do it? He works hard at it. He actually works very hard at it!

If you have a photographic memory, this will be an easy discipline for you. If not, you might need a little help. Fortunately, as with Bible study, excellent tools have been developed to help with Bible memorization. One of the best is The Navigators' *Topical Memory System* (TMS). The TMS features sixty Bible verses dealing with essential issues in the Christian faith. Organized into five topical sets of twelve verses, each set addresses some specific area of Christian growth and discipleship.

For several years I met with small groups of men to nurture our relationships with Jesus. Each group decided to master all sixty of these verses, listening to each other memorize when we met and holding each other accountable. I can't tell you the sense of accomplishment these men felt the day we went through all sixty verses without making one mistake. Here are some of the lessons I learned from those experiences:

1. ***Take small steps.*** Have you seen the movie *What About Bob?* It's a favorite of mine because I am a Bob and because I love Bill Murray. In it, Richard Dreyfuss plays a psychiatrist who has just published a best-selling book called *Baby Steps.* What was true in this goofy movie is true in the area of memorization. For most of us, we need to start by taking baby steps. One verse a week is a suitable goal when you begin to memorize.

2. ***Learn the reference.*** I have friends who can never find the verse they are looking for when they need it. I get phone calls from folks asking me where to find a particular verse. This never happens with my friends who have used the *TMS* because part of the system is memorizing the reference. When you use The Navigators' system, you say the reference *before* you say the verse and you say the reference *after* you say the verse. Over time the reference gets drilled into your memory.

3. ***Review your verses daily.*** Our minds have two fabulous capabilities: the ability to remember *and* the ability to for- get. Once you learn a verse, the theory goes that if you review it by memory fourteen days in a row, you will not for- get it. Again, I have friends who complain that they cannot memorize. They say they memorize a verse but within days they forget it. The problem? They usually aren't reviewing. This leads me to the next tip.

4. ***Memorize with a friend.*** Most of the tough disciplines of life are easier when we do them with a friend. There was a time in my life when I was in very good physical condi- tion. That day is long gone. I *try* to get to the gym. I *try* to get out and walk or jog. But for some time now I have not been getting the job done. In retrospect, the times when I was in great shape were the times I was working out or running with a friend or two. If you build accountability into this discipline, it will help.

Partner with a friend or two and commit together to do something like the *TMS*. Set a time every week when you test each other, either in person or over the phone. Quote the verse you are learning this week, complete with reference and topic. Then go back and quote all the verses from the topic you are working on. This means that by the end of the twelfth week you will be going over twelve verses, some of which you have reviewed the entire time. Then you can move on to the next set of verses.

In all fairness, I have had friends who were "memo- rization challenged." I'm not sure how hard they really worked, but they never seemed to quite pull it off. If you fall into this category, the next tip is for you.

5. ***Keep at it.*** Persistence is one of the great assets in memorization. A management guru once told me most people radically overestimate what they can do in a year, radically underestimate what they can do in five years, and are completely out of touch about what they can accomplish in a lifetime. If you begin to tackle one verse a week, you might not be amazed what you have accomplished at the end of six months. It will take you more than a year just to get through the *TMS*. But if you keep at it, in five years you will have memorized 250 verses. In ten years that number will jump to five hundred. If you exercise that discipline for twenty years, you will have memorized a thousand verses. You could stand up on Sunday morning and quote from memory your pastor's text! That is the power of consistency and persistence.

MEDITATING ON GOD'S WORD

Memorization is not an end in and of itself, but a step in a powerful sequence of internalizing the Word of God. The next step in that sequence, and the second discipline I would challenge you to adopt, is the spiritual discipline of meditation. Let's go back to God's promise in Joshua 1:8: "This book of the law shall not depart from your mouth, but you shall *meditate* on it day and night" (Joshua 1:8 NASB).

Don't let the word *meditate* scare you. I am not going to advocate some strange practice that a foreign guru teaches to help you empty your mind and experience nothingness. That is not the kind of meditation God is instructing Joshua to practice.

Notice that God tells Joshua he is to meditate on the book of the law. This was another name for what we would call the Word of God, or the Bible. In Joshua's day this "book" only contained five documents called the Torah, or Law; those same documents today comprise the first five books of the Old Testament. By the end of Joshua's conquest, the book bearing his name would be added to these five. Over the next fifteen hundred years, book-by-book would be added until we ultimately ended up with the current sixty-six books of Scripture.

God instructed Joshua to meditate on *revealed* truth. It is the things God has spoken and taught that are the source of this kind of meditation. How do you meditate in this manner? Meditation is the thoughtful consideration and reflection we give to a Scripture passage to better understand it. Usually, the objective of medita-tion, as distinguished from study, is to gain a sense of how this particular passage impacts our individual lives.

I was once told that the word picture behind the Hebrew word for *meditate* was that of a cow chewing its cud. The cow chews on the cud for a while and then swallows it. Then the cow regurgi-tates the cud and chews on it some more. I don't know how many times the average cow chews the average cud, but you get the idea. I actually have never been able to verify that the Hebrew word has any relationship to cud-chewing, but it is a colorful way of think-ing about what we do when we meditate on the Scriptures. We chew on it. Then we chew on it some more. Then we come back and chew on it again.

Let's take Joshua's promise from God and do a little medita-tion exercise. We actually have already started. We were meditat-ing when we made the observation that the verse begins with *"This book of the law . . . "*

In meditation we would focus our attention on this phrase and think about it. Our first thought might be that God's instruc-tions include a particular object upon which Joshua is to meditate.

(This is exactly what I pointed out a few paragraphs back.) Then we might ponder exactly what that object was. We ask ourselves the question, *What is the book of the law?*

As we think further, we might remember that the book of Joshua is placed at the end of the first five books of the Old Testament, after leadership has passed from Moses to Joshua. Because Moses is the traditional author of the first five books and because Joshua immediately follows Deuteronomy, the phrase either refers to the first five books of the Bible or specifically to the book of Deuteronomy. Our conclusion might be that if God were to speak to us about meditation today, he might have us think of the whole Bible.

Then we move on to the next phrase: "*. . . shall not depart from your mouth . . .* " Here is a good phrase to chew on. Did Joshua have the Bible in his mouth? Obviously not! Then what does this mean? To put something in your mouth is the first step to internalizing it. In the case of God's Word, this is a good image of mastering the material so that you carry it with you at all times. We have already pointed out that this appears to be a way of speaking about memorization for mastery and internalization. Then comes our next phrase: "*. . . but you shall meditate on it day and night . . .* " Here is our challenge to chew: *Meditate on it day and night.* This is one way of saying that we should be thinking about and reflecting on God's Word throughout the day. Just as we are doing now, think about it for a while. Later on, think about it some more. Ask how your life should be changed by what you have learned from the Bible. Chew, chew, and then chew some more.

In the midst of meditating, your focus should often turn toward personalizing what you are pondering. When you think about not letting the Word depart from your mouth, you might spend some time reflecting on how you are doing in your own memorization. When you think about meditating day and night, you might assess how much of your day is influenced by the Word of God. All of these ways of thinking and reflecting are part of what it means to meditate.

As you memorize verses, spend time carefully thinking about what they say. As bizarre as it might seem, many people memorize and can verbally regurgitate information about which they have little understanding. I think they call it college. This is never the objective with God's Word. You want to know what it means, how it applies to you, and what you can do to implement it in your life.

I have heard speakers talk about how memorization is the key to success. They quote Joshua 1:8. This is not what the verse says. I have heard others say memorization and meditation are the keys to success and prosperity, and again quote this passage. But this is not what this verse says either. It is the *next* step in the process that is the key to success: *". . . so that you may be careful to do according to all that is written in it."*

The final step in the success sequence is the application of God's truth to our daily lives. It is the living of God's Word that brings biblical success and prosperity. That will be the subject of chapter 7's section devoted to enjoying the Bible. For now, note that these two great ways to enjoy the Bible — memorization and meditation — have personal application as their objective. When you put all three of these dynamics to work, enjoyment of the Bible takes on huge new implications. One outcome of this process is a measure of under- standing of and insight into the Bible that will equip you to share with others what you are discovering and experiencing. In the next chapter I will challenge you to enjoy the

Bible by teaching others what you are learning. You cannot believe how much fun this can be and how much it can help you master the Word.

CHAPTER 6
The New Testament Letters

§

UNDERSTANDING THE EPISTLES

Unlike the last chapter, in which we covered only one book of the
New Testament, this chapter covers the sixth major division of the
Bible with its twenty-one documents. These are the letters written by the apostles to the members of the first-century Christian
community. We refer to them as books or epistles, the latter being
another name for a letter. Hang on, because we are going to take
a quick look at all twenty-one!

PART ONE: THE LETTERS OF PAUL

These twenty-one books are often divided into two sections. The
first of these contains the thirteen letters of the apostle Paul and
are appropriately called the Pauline Epistles.

In these letters we are given both theological explanations of
all Christ accomplished on humanity's behalf and practical instructions on how to live the Christian life. If you think of the
Gospels as containing what Jesus did and said, you could think of
the Epistles as explaining what Jesus' work and teaching mean to
us and how to apply these truths in our daily lives.

Ironically, many of these letters were written in response to problems that surfaced in the local churches. Just like today, the church in the first century was filled with challenges because the church *is* people. Where you have people, you will usually have problems. What the Bible teaches is that the problems people have, both individually and corporately, have solutions. The questions we have about living a Christ- centered life have answers.

Paul's letters are arranged together immediately following the book of Acts in the New Testament. The arrangement is neither chronological nor systematic. The letters tend to be organized from the larger to the smaller, beginning with Paul's *magna opus*, the epistle (or letter) to the Romans.

ROMANS

If any of the New Testament letters were designed to give the early church a systematic theology of Christian faith, it would have to be Romans. The comprehensive nature of the letter finds its origins in the historical details surrounding it. Romans is the only letter Paul sent to a gathering of believers that he himself had evidently never visited. Some debate exists over who birthed this particular church, but from Paul's greetings at the end of the letter it is obvious that many of the men and women who had come to faith in Jesus through Paul's ministry were now living in Rome.

Paul knew he had personally taught the fundamental truths of the gospel in other cities, but he was not sure that such a foundation had been laid in Rome. To remedy this potential problem, Paul starts at the very beginning by discussing mankind's rebellion against God.

The first two and a half chapters of Romans develop a theology of fallen humanity. Paul explains that the human race has rejected God's revelation of himself in creation. Paul describes how all people have failed to adequately respond to the conscience God has placed within them and have blatantly broken God's revealed will when it has been made known through prophets and written revelation. The result? Humanity is hopelessly lost, lies in a state of spiritual death, and deserves God's judgment.

Having built a case against humanity, Paul moves on to clearly spell out the only hope men and women have of entering back into a right relationship with God. He tells us that what we were unable to do, God has done. Chapters 3–5 contain a detailed explanation of how Jesus has made it possible not only to be forgiven of sin, but also to actually be declared righteous by God on the basis of what Jesus has done on our behalf. This is the great teaching that theologians refer to as justification by faith. It is the basis of all authentic biblical spirituality. No passage in all the New Testament gives as detailed an explanation of this truth as this one. (Much of what is written here is a thoughtful amplification of Paul's earlier letter to the Galatians, which I'll get to a bit later in this chapter.)

From his explanation of Christ's work in the process of justification, Paul next discusses how that truth plays out in reality. Chapters 6–8 explain how the spiritual life (in other words, a life pleasing to God) is impossible apart from the internal working of the Holy Spirit. Paul instructs the Romans that they are to live according to the Spirit's leading in their lives and to resist the prompting of the old nature, which Paul calls the flesh.

In chapters 9–11 Paul enters into a lengthy theological discussion of God's sovereign purposes as displayed in the history of Israel and the incarnation of Jesus. As will be true in most of Paul's letters, the concluding chapters of Romans (12–16) are filled with specific instructions concerning practical matters of Christian life and faith.

Mastery of the content of Romans is immensely helpful in understanding the rest of the New Testament letters — not only Paul's, but also those by the authors of the General Epistles.

1 CORINTHIANS

Paul's first letter to the church in Corinth follows the book of Romans. Though all of his letters contain theological information, 1 Corinthians was primarily written to address a number of practical problems taking place in the Corinthian fellowship.

Corinth was a wild place. You might compare it to Las Vegas, but that wouldn't quite capture the drama of the city.

"To live like a Corinthian" was actually an ancient expression that meant you were immoral and out of control. It was not easy to faithfully follow Jesus and his teachings in a place like Corinth.

The letter can be divided into the issues Paul addresses and the answers he gives. This was a group of believers that began to fragment along personality lines. Some identified with Paul, others with Peter (Cephas), still others with the orator Apollos. These petty arguments were divisive, and Paul told his readers they were acting like people who had never had an encounter with Jesus. Chapters 1–6 address this issue.

The Corinthian culture was also known for its litigious nature. Going to court was almost a sporting event in Corinth. Consequently, brothers and sisters in the faith were constantly suing one another. Paul wrote that they were better off being wronged than dragging the name of Jesus through the public mud. Chapter 6 addresses this issue.

Corinth was infamous for its immorality. The preeminent edifice in the city was the temple of Aphrodite, which adorned the Acropolis. One thousand sacred prostitutes serviced this temple, and every night these women would descend to work the city streets. Another saying from the ancient world was, "Not every man can afford a trip to Corinth!"

Immorality was likewise a problem in the church. Some Corinthian believers were still having sexual relationships with the prostitutes. Paul had to remind them that because they were now living in spiritual union with Jesus, it was as if they were making Christ have sex with prostitutes. We usually make it sound much more religious than this in our sermons, but that is the bottom line of Paul's letter.

The church also experienced problems during its times of corporate worship, abusing the agape feast, or what we now call communion. In Paul's time this meal was like a modern potluck dinner. Everyone brought something to share. But in Corinth, those with food and wine were not sharing with those less fortunate. The prosperous were going home drunk and stuffed while the poor went away hungry.

The inappropriate use of spiritual gifts, especially the gift of tongues, was another issue. Paul summarized the problem by saying the Corinthian church services were doing more harm than good. The good news for you and me is that in addressing these problems this letter gives us a marvelous explanation of the role of spiritual gifts in our contemporary spiritual adventure (chapters 12–14).

Finally, some Corinthians did not believe that those who had already died would be resurrected. In chapter 15, Paul not only corrected them, but also gave a lengthy theology of resurrection. He noted that more than five hundred people, many of who were still alive as Paul wrote, saw the resurrected Christ.

2 CORINTHIANS

The second letter to the Corinthians was a sequel to the first. One of the problems tackled in the first letter was so severe that Paul recommended throwing the offending person out of the church. Now he writes to encourage the Corinthians to bring the repentant member back into the fellowship.

Second Corinthians is a very personal letter. By the time Paul wrote it, his authority in the church was being questioned by some. As a result, Paul wrote about his ministry and the issues that should be evaluated when deciding whether or not his authority was valid. He speaks of how God makes himself known through weak and faulty human vessels. He teaches that dependence on Christ is the source of true strength. He acknowledges that this earthly body is temporary and that God has prepared an eternal place with Jesus where we go immediately upon physical death.

One of the highlights of the book is Paul's description of personally having been taken into the presence of God (12:1-4). Paul saw what lies ahead for those who know and love God. It was this experience that shaped his attitudes about life and death, reflected in letters such as Philippians, where he wrote, "I desire to depart [die] and be with Christ, which is better by far [than life]" (Philippians 1:23).

GALATIANS

Although the letter to the Galatians is located after the Corinthian and Romans letters, it preceded them chronologically. It is possible that Galatians is actually the earliest New Testament document, though the general epistle of James competes for this honor. Both appear to have been written as early as 45–50 A.D.

Galatia was the region where Paul spent most of his first missionary journey, as recorded in Acts 13–14. It seems that wherever Paul went he was followed by Jewish teachers from Jerusalem who tried to convince non-Jewish converts that they also had to become Jewish. Their message, unlike Paul's, was that faith in Christ and his death on the cross was only part of what produced a right relationship with God. They taught that men needed to be circumcised according to the Jewish law and to keep the law of Moses. Paul wrote Galatians to combat this error. It is the classic instruction on the relationship between faith in what God has done for us and what we are able to do through our own efforts.

Using some of the strongest language in the New Testament, Paul writes that the ones who are teaching a message different from his should be *anathema,* or damned eternally. He also explains how the authority to preach this message did not come from human agency, but from his call to apostleship, given by Jesus himself.

In one of the Bible's more revealing passages, Paul tells of a conflict he had with Peter over these issues. The human tendency to give preference to those who most agree with our position became a source of hypocrisy in the church. Peter began to withdraw from non-Jewish Christians in social situations such as table fellowship. Paul confronted him: "We who are Jews by birth, and not gentile 'sinners' know that a man is not justified by his human efforts, but through faith in what Jesus has done. How is it then that you are trying to force Gentiles to act like Jews?" (2:14-25, free translation from the Greek text).

Galatians uses many arguments to show that faith in Jesus and the gift of the Spirit are the keys to authentically belonging to and following Christ. Galatians 5 contains Paul's explanation of the struggle we experience when our old nature — what Paul calls the flesh, or sinful nature — and our new nature, created by the holy Spirit's presence in our lives, come into conflict. In this same chapter Paul also gives his great analysis of the outcome of living under the dominant influence of either of these two internal realities. Our lives either bear the "works of the flesh" or the "fruit of the Spirit." Galatians teaches us that human religiosity is not the objective of biblical spirituality. Living under the dominant influence of the Spirit and allowing our lives to be transformed from the inside out is what counts.

EPHESIANS

Galatians is followed in our Bibles by Ephesians. Ephesians is one of three letters written by Paul around 60 A.D. while under house arrest in Rome. These three are called the Prison Epistles because of their place of origin.

Ephesus was one of the major cities of the Roman province of Asia Minor. Today the location is part of modern Turkey. The archaeological excavations at Ephesus are some of the greatest from the ancient world.

Paul spent a great deal of time in Ephesus on his third missionary journey (see Acts 19). Unlike places like Thessalonica, where he only stayed for days, Paul spent two to three years in Ephesus. As a result, the message of Jesus spread through- out Asia Minor. The seven churches addressed in the book of Revelation were products of this period of Paul's ministry.

Ephesians seems much more like a letter written to solid followers of Christ than a corrective combating false teaching and poor behavior. It is as if Paul is writing these dear friends and calling them to a higher level of spiritual experience. As such, it is one of the most challenging letters of the New Testament.

In the early chapters Paul spends a great deal of time reminding the Ephesians of all that is involved in being united with Christ. Authentic biblical spirituality is more than experiencing Christ in us. It is being raised up and seated with Christ in the heavenlies (2:6). Someday I hope to understand what that really means!

The second half of the letter (chapters 4–6) is a call to respond to the lofty truths of the first half. Paul begins by challenging the believers in Ephesus to "live a life worthy of the calling you have received" (4:1).

Among his more than fifty specific exhortations, Paul instructs the Ephesians that they are to be filled with the Spirit (5:18), rid themselves of all anger and rage (4:31), speak the truth in love (4:15), discover and do God's will (5:17), stop using language in abusive ways (4:29), imitate God (5:1), submit to one another in love (5:21), and put on right behavior as if it were a suit of armor (6:10-12). These extremely challenging chapters form a "must-study" section for anyone wanting to know how to live in a way that pleases God.

PHILIPPIANS

The book of Philippians is another of the Prison Epistles, one that Paul wrote as a thank-you letter for a gift of support sent to him by the church at Philippi. Philippians has often been called the Epistle of Joy because of that recurring theme. However, I have come to believe that Jesus, not joy, is the primary message of the book. The word *joy* or *rejoice* is used some seven times in these four short chapters, but the name Jesus appears over twenty times. When our focus is on Jesus, joy will follow, regardless of our circumstances.

This letter, like Ephesians, was written late in Paul's ministry. At the time, Paul himself had been in relationship with Jesus some twenty-five years. He also was in a life-threatening situation, facing trial and possible death at the hands of the Roman emperor Nero. Written to some of his closest friends to encourage them in their spiritual lives, Philippians offers an intimate glimpse into the heart of the apostle.

The first chapter of Philippians explains the details of Paul's situation. It is also famous for Paul's evaluation that dying and being with Jesus is better than living. Here he makes his famous declaration, "For to me, to live is Christ and to die is gain" (verse 21).

In the second chapter Paul encouraged the Philippians to choose a life of humility, using the example of Christ himself to challenge them. This is the text where Paul talks about the *kenosis*, or emptying, of Jesus in his incarnation and crucifixion. The way of the cross was, for Paul, a way of descent. Only with this kind of attitude could the church live in harmony and fulfill its God-given purpose.

Philippians 3 contains a bit of Paul's autobiography. We learn that he had attained all that the ancient Jewish world viewed as a means of righteousness and a measure of success. We also learn that his faith in Jesus resulted in the loss of all these things. Yet Paul viewed his many accomplishments as *skubala* compared to all he had gained through Christ. The translation of this Greek word has several possibilities. Most modern versions use the word *rubbish*, but the King James Version was probably more accurate in translating it *dung*. You get the idea.

Paul ends this letter with a call for believers to be united in fellowship, to adopt a spirit of rejoicing, and to let their minds dwell on the pure and lovely things of life (4:1-8).

COLOSSIANS

Paul wrote the letter to the Colossians to combat one of the early theological errors the church repeatedly confronted. Although still in its incipient form, the error involved an attempt by some to view the gospel through the lens of a Greek philosophy eventually called Gnosticism. The word comes from the Greek *gnosis*, meaning "knowledge." Gnosticism was a type of mystery religion advocating salvation through the acquisition of knowledge only possessed by the initiated elite.

The main thrust of Colossians concerns the true nature of Jesus Christ. The Gnostics taught a theory of dualism in which spirit was considered good and matter was considered evil. As such, these early teachers tended to deny the incarnation of Jesus. Some taught that Jesus only appeared to have a body, but was actually pure spirit. In its extreme form Gnosticism taught that there was a difference between the divine Christ and the human Jesus. Some suggested that the divine Christ merely "rested" on the human Jesus, but departed prior to the Crucifixion. In the spurious second-century "gospel of Thomas," the author (not actually Thomas, but someone using the name to gain credibility) depicts "The Christ" sitting with Thomas in a cave watching the Crucifixion from afar. To counter this lie Paul taught that *all* the fullness of God was present in Jesus by virtue of his deity (1:19; 2:9). He is the God-Man, fully human and fully divine.

The second half of Colossians tackles the practical issues that the Gnostic teaching was creating in the church. Those who held to theological dualism tended to go in one of two directions. Some practiced an extreme asceticism that viewed spirituality as primarily a process of physical denial and abuse. Others argued that because spirit and matter were separate, it did not matter what one did in the body. This produced an antinomian (against law) doctrine that at times actually viewed spirituality as a product of violating the laws of the God of the Old Testament, who was viewed as an inferior deity who had made a mistake when he created the world.

In response to these extremes Paul wrote about living a disciplined life in the Spirit. He again articulated how a life of following Jesus ought to look. It is not a matter of external issues but one of loving Christ and being led by the Spirit. It is a holistic venture in which what we do in the body is a reflection of what Jesus is doing in our inner life.

1 THESSALONIANS

First Thessalonians was one of Paul's earlier letters, written to a church planted on a brief stop during his second missionary journey. Concerned about their spiritual welfare, Paul had sent his traveling companion Timothy to check on them. Timothy had returned to Paul with a good report. Paul wrote both to encourage and to instruct the Thessalonians, reminding them of their time together and his joy in hearing of their progress in the faith.

One of the better-known sections of this letter is found in the fourth chapter. During his time in Thessalonica, Paul had apparently taught the church about the return of Jesus. He did such a good job of impressing them with the imminent nature of this event that they were concerned about what was going to happen to those who had died since they were last with Paul. Would they also be with Jesus? In response Paul wrote about the time when Jesus comes and takes his followers to be with him. "The dead in Christ will rise first," Paul affirms (4:16). Then those who are still alive will be "caught up" with them in the clouds to meet the Lord in the air (4:17). This event has become known as the rapture.

2 THESSALONIANS

This end-times theme seems to have been a major issue in Thessalonica. Paul's second letter to the believers there appears to have been stimulated by reports that some were teaching that the Day of the Lord had already come. In response, Paul gave more detail concerning those events that must precede the second coming of Christ, emphasizing the appearance of the one we have come to identify as the Antichrist. Paul calls him "the man of lawlessness" (2:1-4). he writes that "the restrainer" is currently holding back the arrival of this person, but a day is coming when this restrainer will be removed and the Antichrist will come (2:7). For centuries theologians have argued about who or what this restrainer is. Paul knew. We don't.

The rest of the letter is an exhortation to positive living in light of the fact that these things will happen in God's perfect timing. Paul's main challenge is that the readers "stand firm" in the faith (2:15).

THE PASTORAL EPISTLES (1–2 TIMOTHY AND TITUS)

The final letters of Paul contained in our New Testament include what are often called the Pastoral Epistles. This title reflects the fact that rather than being written to a group of believers, the letters were to individuals that Paul had placed in positions of pastoral leadership in local fellowships.

Two of these letters were written to Paul's young apprentice Timothy. Timothy came from Derbe in the region of Galatia and joined Paul on his second missionary expedition. He became like a son to the apostle and was certainly a son in the faith.

Timothy often accompanied Paul on his ministry trips. On one of these expeditions Paul left Timothy in Ephesus. Timothy's job was to keep the church on track by combating false teaching (1 Timothy 1:3). If you are beginning to think that the problem of false teaching was rampant in the early church, you are correct. Most histories of the early years of the Christian church show how much of what we today think of as orthodox theology was forged in the crucible of refuting false doctrine.

These letters to Timothy are intensely personal. Paul encourages his protégé to help lead the church by teaching sound doctrine and living a life that exemplifies what he teaches. The first letter is filled with instructions concerning *what* Timothy is to teach. He is to teach against those who are sidetracked by "myths and endless genealogies" (1:4). He is to encourage the church in a life of prayer (2:1-8). He is instructed about what character qualities to look for in a church leader (3:1-12). He is told how to care for the widows in the fellowship (5:1-16) and what a believer's attitude toward money should be (6:3-10). Finally, Paul exhorts Timothy to pursue a life pleasing to Jesus (6:11-16).

The second letter to Timothy has quite a different tone. Believed by many scholars to be Paul's final letter, it was written from prison, but not the same imprisonment during which the earlier Prison Epistles were penned. This was Paul's final imprisonment before being beheaded, and he likely was held in the dungeon of Rome's infamous Mamertine Prison. You can visit this site today and see the place many believe was Paul's "home" during this period. This letter served as a farewell charge to young

Timothy and includes Paul's famous assessment of his life and ministry: "I have fought the good fight, I have finished the race, I have kept the faith" (4:7).

The third letter of the Pastoral Epistles was written to another of Paul's protégés, Titus. Titus had been given a challenging ministry assignment: he was left on the island of Crete to "straighten out what was left unfinished and appoint elders in every town" (1:5). This must have been a bit difficult, because Paul confirms the truth of the adage, "Cretans are always liars, evil brutes, lazy gluttons" (1:12).

This short letter contains two great passages. One is the encouragement to live in a way that pleases God while we wait for "the blessed hope — the glorious appearing of our great God and Savior, Jesus Christ" (2:12-13). The other is the declaration that God "saved us, not because of righteous things we had done, but because of his mercy" (3:5).

PHILEMON

The final letter of Paul is written to his friend Philemon. It is not really a pastoral letter in the sense of being written to a pastor, but one written on behalf of Philemon's slave Onesimus.

The letter indicates that Onesimus ran away from Philemon and ended up in Rome. While there, Onesimus met Paul, who led him to faith. Now Paul is sending Onesimus back to Philemon, not as a slave, but as a brother in Christ. He urges Philemon to forgive Onesimus the wrong he has done and embrace him as a fellow follower of Jesus. Paul definitely asserts some of his pastoral clout by reminding Philemon, ". . . not to mention that you owe me your very self" (verse 19).

Part Two: The General Epistles

Hebrews

Hebrews is the first of what are called the General Epistles, which simply means they were written by someone other than Paul. This section of the New Testament contains eight documents by five different authors.

We do not know who wrote the book of Hebrews. The document itself is untitled. It does not begin in standard epistolary form either, so the recipients are also a matter of speculation. The letter's closing remarks tell us that the writer was a friend of Timothy and is in the company of friends of the recipients "from Italy" (13:23-24). Because of these remarks, some have suggested that Paul is the author. The document also is consistent with Paul's theology and uses some of Paul's common phrases, words, and concepts.

On the other hand, the letter is quite different from the rest of Paul's epistles. Because of this, it has been suggested that perhaps it was one of Paul's associates or ministry partners that wrote the letter. One fascinating theory is that the early church leader Priscilla was the author and left it unsigned because of fear that the church would question the authority of a woman. Others have suggested that the teacher Apollos was the author because of the letter's scholarly manner.

The recipients have several identifiable characteristics. They seem to live in Italy, probably Rome. (Most believe the writer is outside Italy, sending greetings back to Rome.) The recipients appear to have a Jewish background. They are definitely having a tough time. The author writes to encourage these believers to resist the temptation to revert to Judaism and abandon Christ.

Hebrews is an apologetic letter. It seeks to build a defense for the superiority of the New Covenant over the Old Covenant and argues that a return to Judaism is a major step in the wrong direction. Using an extensive understanding of the Old Testament, the writer shows how Christ is the fulfillment of all that the Old Covenant attempted to accomplish, and he is the solution to the problems the "Hebrews" are experiencing.

The discouraged and distressed recipients have lost sight of who Christ is. In response the author builds a case for the superiority of Jesus to angels (chapters 1–2), to Moses (chapter 3), and to the high priest of Israel (chapters 4–8). In light of these truths he or she exhorts the Hebrews to fix their *thoughts* on Jesus to correct their false thinking (3:1), and to fix their *eyes* on Jesus to get their focus back in the proper place (12:2).

The writer contrasts the Old Testament sacrificial system with the once-for-all sacrifice of Jesus, which cannot be improved upon. He or she gives a marvelous explanation of the significance of Jesus being a priest in the lineage of the mysterious character Melchizedek. One of the great chapters of the New Testament is Hebrews 11, in which the writer encourages his readers by painting a word picture of the Faith Hall of Fame.

JAMES

Hebrews is followed in the New Testament lineup by the book of James. James was a leader of the Jerusalem church during the early days of apostolic history. He was not the apostle James. Tradition tells us this James was the half-brother of Jesus Christ. Paul refers to him as "the Lord's brother" in the letter to the Galatians (1:19).

James is considered the earliest of the General Epistles. It can be dated around the same time that Paul wrote Galatians, about 45–50 A.D. The letter was written to Jews who had come to faith in Jesus and is even addressed to "the twelve tribes scattered among the nations" (1:1).

The main thrust of James is an exhortation to live consistently with one's faith as a demonstration that, in fact, one *has* an authentic faith. It is so filled with instructions about behavior, and contains so little emphasis on the work of Christ or the power of the Spirit, that at times the inclusion of the letter in the canon has been challenged. Martin Luther called it "an epistle of straw" and suggested it be removed from the Bible.

If you step back and look at the big picture, you can see how God would want a letter like James to be included in the New Testament. It serves to keep a letter like Galatians from being misused and misinterpreted. Paul says we are saved by faith apart from works. James balances by saying authentic faith will manifest itself in action. Paul says it is for freedom that Christ has set us free. James says we must submit ourselves to God.

1–2 Peter

First Peter is another letter written primarily to a Jewish–Christian audience. Peter addresses them as "God's elect" and lists the regions of the ancient world to which they had been "scattered." Some suggest this letter was written after one of the early persecutions recorded in Acts, when believers from Jerusalem were scattered around the Roman Empire.

Peter was writing to encourage these victims of Persecution. He recognized that for a short while they "may have had to suffer grief in all kinds of trials" (1:6). Despite their trials, he admonished them to "be holy, because I [God] am holy" (1:16; see Leviticus 11:44).

The middle chapters of the letter include a series of instructions concerning relationships. Chapter 3 contains one of the more helpful sections on husband-and-wife relationships. Wives are to be submissive, gentle, and quiet-spirited. Husbands are to be gentle and considerate of their wives. Together they are to live as "heirs . . . of the gracious gift of life" (3:7). Peter sums this section up by saying that all of us are to live in harmony with one another and be sympathetic, loving, compassionate, and humble (3:8).

Peter's second letter has a more specific focus: addressing problems regarding false teachers. Peter begins by asserting the authority of his message. It was not a "cleverly invented" story, but a prophecy of Scripture, spoken by men inspired by the Holy Spirit (1:16-21). This would seem to suggest that the false teachers had deviated from the Scriptures and had introduced what Peter calls "destructive heresies" (2:1). Peter's comments on these teachers indicate that they were using the theology of grace in a way that led to what has been called "cheap grace." He says, "with eyes full of adultery, they never stop sinning; they seduce the unstable; they are experts in greed — an accursed brood!" (2:14). The kind of freedom they taught was nothing more than an appeal to the flesh. Peter compares the behavior stimulated by this false teaching to a dog returning to eat its vomit (2:22). Not a pretty picture!

Peter ends this letter with a reminder of the destiny of the human race. Though some might ridicule the teaching that Jesus is coming again, it doesn't change the fact that he is. The Day of the Lord is going to come in a very surprising manner. This truth should motivate followers of Jesus to live wholesomely and expectantly (3:3-14).

1–3 JOHN

The next three books of the New Testament are brief letters written by the apostle John. They are usually dated quite late and are considered among the last documents of the canon. The first of these letters is significantly longer than the other two and was written to the larger church body. In it John sets out a series of tests of Christian authenticity.

As he did in the gospel he wrote at a later date and, as in the book of Revelation, John uses imagery to get his points across. He encourages his audience to "walk in the light" (1:7) and says that authentic spirituality will create a change in our behavior that moves us from "darkness" into "light." John teaches that love is the essential mark of spiritual authenticity. Loving our brothers and sisters in Christ is evidence that we are living in the light. If we claim to have encountered Jesus, yet still don't love, there is reason to question the authenticity of our faith. Someone has said that the message of 1 John is to "keep the main thing the main thing." The main thing, according to John, is loving God and loving one another.

Like Paul and Peter, John warns against the presence of false teachers in the midst of the church. John calls them "antichrists" (2:18). He tells his readers that they need to develop discernment to be able to "test the spirits" and distinguish between false teachers and the genuine article (4:1).

The final chapter of 1 John contains one of the great statements concerning Christian assurance. How can a person be sure he has eternal life? John makes it clear: "And this is the testimony: God has given us eternal life, and this life is in his Son. He who has the Son has life; he who does not have the Son of God does not have life" (5:11-12).

The second of John's letters is addressed to "the chosen lady and her children" (1:1). Scholars believe that John was speaking here of one of the churches of Asia Minor over which he had spiritual oversight. He even addresses himself as "the elder" in the same verse.

Second John is a warning against the same heresy Paul addressed in his letter to the Colossians. As was true in Colossae, teachers with Gnostic leanings were denying the incarnation of Jesus. This was a common trend in a form of Gnosticism called Docetism, which taught that Jesus only appeared to have a body but was actually pure spirit. (The name Docetism comes from the Greek "to appear.") John warns that such teachers should not be allowed to speak in the churches.

John's third and final letter is addressed to his friend Gaius. It is both a note of encouragement and a warning. Gaius had been showing hospitality to traveling teachers sent out by the church at Ephesus. For this, John encouraged and commended him.

On the other hand, there was a leader in Gaius's church who was creating problems for John. His name was Diotrephes, and he had an ego problem. John says he "loves to be first" (verse 9). Not only did Diotrephes resist the call to help traveling ministers, but he actually forbade others to practice such hospitality. This same man was speaking maliciously about those John identifies as "us," a possible reference to the leadership of the church in the region.

JUDE
The final document of the General Epistles is a short letter written by Jude. Jude identifies himself as a brother of James. The most likely explanation of this description is that Jude was also a half-brother of Jesus. Like many other New Testament letter writers, Jude wrote to combat doctrinal error.

Though Jude says he originally intended to write other things, he felt compelled to urge his audience to "contend for the faith that was once for all entrusted to the saints" (verse 3). He goes on to explain that false teachers had infiltrated the church with a false application of the principle of grace. Specifically, Jude said they were turning grace into a "license for immorality" (verse 4).

Jude clearly states that God will judge these false teachers for their destructive influence. To those within the church he writes words of encouragement, challenging them to build themselves up in the faith and not to be led astray by these men.

Jude ends with a doxology worthy to be the doxology for all these wonderful Epistles, inspired and preserved by the Holy Spirit for the encouragement and instruction of Christ's followers through the centuries: "To him who is able to keep you from falling and to present you before his glorious presence without fault and with great joy — to the only God our Savior be glory, majesty, power and authority, through Jesus Christ our Lord, before all ages, now and forevermore! Amen." (verses 24-25).

ENJOYING THE BIBLE: TEACHING THE WORD
It has been over forty years since I first stood in front of a classroom and attempted to communicate something of what I was learning

about the Bible. Since that day I have been privileged to tell thousands of men and women what the Bible says and how it can help us live God's way. For nearly thirty years I have devoted myself to teaching the Bible in full-time vocational Christian ministry. I am a teacher. Actually, I am a human being who happens to teach, but that is another subject.

I have taught some relatively large groups of men and women during those years, but that first group was the toughest. It was the kindergarten Sunday school class at Colonial Presbyterian Church in Kansas City, Missouri. I was a very young believer at the time and wanted to find a way to serve Jesus. There was a need and I filled it.

I was not a very good kindergarten Sunday school teacher. For one thing, most of the students already knew more about the Bible than I did. For another, I wasn't adept at keeping a room full of five-year-olds under control. I also discovered that the lecture method is not very effective with this age group.

I finally surrendered and simply shouted out verses, claiming the promise of Isaiah that God's Word never returns to him void, while thirty young "ankle biters" climbed all over me. I share this story to let you know that we all start somewhere. At some point in time you probably will find yourself in a situation where you become the teacher. This might be as simple as teaching your own children something about the Bible or as complex as taking on a teaching ministry.

It wasn't long after the kindergarten Sunday school experience that I got my second teaching opportunity. This time it was with a group of college students I belonged to. Things went better with the college students. I seemed to be able to communicate with them in a way that made sense and appeared helpful. During that time I sensed a call to a teaching ministry. I had never read the Bible before my conversion. Now I found myself extremely interested in understanding this amazing book. I would read the Bible for hours at a time. Sometimes I found myself falling behind in my college classes because I was studying the Bible more than my textbooks.

By the time I graduated I was convinced that God wanted me to accept a youth minister position in Holdrege, Nebraska, that had been offered to me. I was so green behind the ears spiritually that even now I am grateful that I didn't make more mistakes than I did.

Once I settled into my new job, I went to a Christian bookstore and bought about a dozen small Bible-study booklets to use in developing lessons for our kids. I would take the general outline of one of these studies and use it as a guideline in preparing my own material. But after several months I grew dissatisfied with this technique. What I really wanted was to share with these students what I felt God was teaching me from my own study. I wanted to be original.

I once read a great quote from John Wesley that describes how I began to tackle my teaching work:

> *I sit down alone, only God is here;*
> *In his presence I open, I read his books; And what I thus learn,*
> *I teach.*

I have been following this formula ever since.

As I began to take what I was learning in my study and communicate it to these students, God began to use what I was sharing to help them grow in their relationships with Jesus. How cool is that?!

BECOMING A TEACHER

After several years in Nebraska I felt the need to get a better theological education. To accomplish this I moved to Denver, Colorado, with my wife, Allison, and enrolled at Denver Seminary. I ended up spending nearly nine years as a student there and completed both a master's degree and a doctorate. Early in my seminary experience I was taught the three essential elements in any act of effective communication: *pathos, logos, and ethos.*

First, effective communication involves *pathos.* This is one of the Greek words for emotion, from which we get our word *passion.* A good communicator is passionate about the subject matter he is teaching. We all have had good teachers and we all have had bad teachers. Often the ingredient that makes the difference between the two is *pathos.*

I love the Bible. I believe it is the inspired Word of God. When I read it, I sense God speaking to me. When I teach it, I often sense God speaking through me. This gets me excited. Often it gets me too excited. I have numerous faults as a communicator. One is that I am loud. Fortunately, I am so loud that I can even teach a crowd when the sound system is not working properly. And just as fortunate, when I am using a sound system, the people running it can turn me down.

I also speak rapidly — what one of my friends used to call my machine-gun approach. I get excited about what I am teaching and when I am excited I get loud and I get fast! (Over the years I have slowed down a bit and it has made me a better communicator.)

My point is that if the Bible does not excite and thrill you, maybe you would be better off not doing this assignment. Remember the quote I used earlier in the book about it being a "sin to bore a kid with Christ"? If *pathos* for God's Word is missing in your life, pray that God would give it to you.

Think about it! The Bible is no ordinary book. These are not ordinary facts that we are communicating. This is a message from the living God, inspired by the Holy Spirit, having the potential to change lives for all eternity! When I speak these things, by the work of the Holy Spirit, God can use me as an instrument of his purposes.

I never worry if people leave the church without totally absorbing all the material I have taught. Most of us need to hear information a number of times before we really master it. But if people leave unexcited about the Bible, then maybe I have failed. Maybe I have not taught with enough *pathos*. *Pathos* is contagious!

Pathos is important, but it is not enough. I remember my theology professor, Bruce Demarest, often responding to students' impassioned appeals about theological matters by simply saying, "keen . . . but clueless!" The second element of effective communication of God's Word is *logos*. *Logos* has to do with the actual content of the teaching. Be sure that what you are teaching is accurate and true. This requires disciplined preparation. In chapters 3 and 4 we looked at various steps in studying the Bible. Study is the work that yields your *logos*. You not only want to be impassioned about your teaching, you also want to be informed.

The Bible is a book that requires a lifetime of study. The deeper you dig into a passage, the more truth it will yield. You can give a decent message without a great deal of preparation. A message might only have one or two pieces of information you are attempting to communicate. But you cannot *teach* well without significant preparation. Teaching usually involves communicating a significant body of information. This is especially true if you desire to teach the entire Bible.

On March 9, 1982, I began teaching an adult class at Cherry Hills Community Church in Denver. On that first Sunday I started in the first chapter of Genesis. Except for vacations and those Sundays on which I preached, I taught every Sunday for the next fifteen years. When I left Cherry Hills in June 1997, I had still not taught through the entire Bible! If you are going to teach the Bible, you have a lifetime of material to communicate!

The first *logos* decision a teacher has to make is what he is going to teach. Because I teach consecutively through books of the Bible, my first decision comes when I am starting a new series. I ask God what book I should teach in that particular context. Often he leads me to teach what I am studying in my own devotional time.

Once the general book has been determined, a teacher needs to figure out how much to bite off in any one teaching experience. This is not always easy. When I first started work on this book I was teaching a Wednesday evening study in the book of Galatians. One week I made it through two verses: Galatians 2:15-16. These verses are so filled with theological significance I felt I needed to devote the entire session to them alone.

Another week I taught through an entire chapter. By the end of the session I knew I had bitten off too much material. As you become more accustomed to teaching you will begin to sense how much you can handle in the time allotted.

Next, go through a process much like outlining a chapter in Bible study. Determine the main point you think God is trying to get across in the passage and make that the thrust of your teaching. Some teachers use a method called expository teaching. This usually means going verse by verse through the text. If this is the technique you find most helpful, decide how many verses you can tackle and the main point of those verses.

I use a modified form of expository preaching/teaching. Because the chapter and verse numbers were later additions and not part of the original text, I try to break down the book into "thought blocks." I look for a section of text in which one main thought is taught. At times this will be a very short block of text, at other times it might be more extensive. In either case, your first question ought to be, "What is the text saying?" When your students leave your teaching session, this one point is what you want to be sure they take with them. I call these big ideas "take aways".

After identifying the main point of the text, discover how the writer develops this point. For instance, if the writer sup- ports the main point by giving three illustrations, these illustrations might be your three sub-points. Let's use Philippians 3 again as an example of this process in action.

Studying the first eleven verses, we find the main point to be that Paul's value system was radically changed by his relationship with Jesus. Paul developed this theme by working through three distinct phases of his value formation. He described his old values by listing his many former accomplishments and credentials (your first sub-point). He then evaluated those accomplishments by assessing how their loss compared to knowing Christ (your second sub-point). Finally, Paul identified the substance of his new set of values (your third sub-point).

Now that you have a game plan on what and how to teach, it's time to put meat on the bones. Your study led you to examine many items in this passage. Perhaps you have studied the significance of the seven credentials Paul mentions. Or you have done a word study to understand just what Paul meant when he called his accomplishments "rubbish" compared to knowing Christ. Or you've gotten a better grasp of the word *know* as Paul uses it in the phrase, "I want to know Christ." By now you have also done a historical study of Philippians and are aware of how long Paul has known Jesus and that he was writing these things from prison. All this information can add to the effectiveness of your teaching. If you have a gift for teaching, by the time you begin to see all these various elements come together you will probably be getting excited about the passage. You have been building both *logos* and *pathos.*

When the time comes actually to teach your class or group or even your family, you might begin by telling them how much you enjoyed studying this portion of Scripture. During this introduction you could reflect on how we all struggle with having the kind of values God wants us to have. Then you might observe how fortunate it is that God has given us a model in the apostle Paul. Describe how his value system went through a process of transformation that included three stages. Finally, inform your students that it is these three stages you intend to explore with them.

If you have passion for the Word and diligently prepare, delivery becomes something you work on every time you teach. If you have never taught before, you might find it difficult at first and want to give up. This is natural. Most of the excellent teachers and communicators I know have felt like this. I still experience this feeling when it seems I didn't do the material justice. Here are three important tips to remember:

First, before you teach, or even prepare to teach, ask the Holy Spirit to guide and use you. Invite him to be so in control of your life that you will be his instrument in the lives of your class. If you do not understand what I have just said, you might want to read my book on the Holy Spirit before you attempt to become a teacher. (Available on Amazon.com).

Second, if you stick to the Bible, your work will not be in vain. God uses his Word in people's lives. Share your heart. Share what God has taught you. Keep drawing the class back to the text. Suggest that they read it on their own during the week and challenge them to memorize a central verse. Your greatest job is to get people to interact with the Scriptures. God can use our feeble efforts in ways we are usually oblivious to.

Third, my most important piece of advice is to give teaching a chance. Somehow find a way to share what you are learning from the Word. You might not teach in a formal setting, but you *can* be a teacher. The writer of Hebrews says, "By this time you ought to be teachers" (5:12). In other words, truth is to be shared. If we simply keep taking it in, we will become spiritually stagnant.

Several years ago I took a dip in the Dead Sea. The Dead Sea has a very famous water source — the Jordan River. Running south from the Sea of Galilee, it provides fresh water that irrigates the entire Jordan valley and gives life to all it touches. Then it runs into the Dead Sea. The area around and south of the Dead Sea is desert. The Dead Sea itself cannot sustain life; it is stagnant. Why? It has no outlet. Fresh water enters the sea and sits until it becomes stagnant.

I think God might have put the Dead Sea right where he did to teach a special spiritual principle. We need to give away what God gives us. If we simply take and take, that which God gives becomes stagnant. This is true of all our resources. If God blesses us materially, we are called to share. If we don't, our possessions possess us and we become spiritually stagnant. The same is true with the truth. I know many lovely men and women who have been in the church for years and years. They receive week after week. Sometimes they are in two or three Bible studies a week. They are on information overload. Their problem is that they never do anything with what they have learned. They don't share the truth. Often, they stagnate.

So here is my challenge: look for ways to become a teacher of the Word. Give it a try. Step out in faith. You might be surprised at what you discover.

This brings us to the third element of effective communication. It is called *ethos*. *Ethos* has to do with the character or life of the communicator. We will explore this dimension in the next chapter.

CHAPTER 7

The Book of Revelation

§

Understanding Revelation

OUR FINAL DIVISION OF THE Bible contains a single book. Most of us know this document by the title "Revelation," though in some versions it's called "The Apocalypse", or "The Apocalypse of John".

The word *apocalypse* is a transliteration of the original Greek word *apocalupsis*, meaning an "unveiling" or revealing of that which cannot be known by mere human reasoning. In this book, Jesus Christ reveals the events leading up to his triumphant return to planet Earth and the consummation of all human history.

For many, the book of Revelation seems confusing and complicated, so they avoid studying it. This is unfortunate. In some ways, it is actually a very simple book to understand, once you know a few important facts.

The first fact is tied to the title of the book. An *apocalupsis* was a form of literature quite common to John's first- century audience and totally foreign to ours. In apocalyptic documents, future events are typically portrayed in very symbolic language. The key to understanding the message is to know what the symbols represent.

For most of us, an initial reading of Revelation is totally baffling. After all, what in the world are all these beasts and horns and scrolls and thrones about? What does it mean that 144,000 of the twelve tribes get sealed? Who are the two witnesses? What are we to think of a woman with the sun and the moon and twelve stars around her head? To a modern reader it seems incomprehensible. To John's audience, it made perfect sense.

Apocalyptic literature had a code. In the case of Revelation, the code was the Old Testament. Every symbol used in Revelation is related to a particular Old Testament passage. If you know the Old Testament, you know the code. John's audience knew the code.

The message of this book is also intimately tied to the historical circumstances that led to its writing. As probably the last New Testament document to be written, most scholars date it around 95 A.D. By now, John was an old man and the last of the original apostles still living. He wrote at a time of personal difficulty for both himself and the apostolic church.

The character of the man who sat on the Roman throne often dictated the circumstances of the early church. When the emperor was sympathetic to the Christian community, times tended to be good. When the emperor was hostile, times were difficult. The latter became the case in 81 A.D., when an emperor named Domitian ascended the throne.

Roman religion was characterized by a multiplicity of deities. Indeed, there were so many gods in the Roman pantheon that they built altars to an "unknown god" just to cover all the bases (Acts 17:23). One of the deities of the Roman religious system was the emperor himself. From the time of Augustus, the concept of the divine origin of the emperor was common dogma.

Historically, it would seem that some emperors, like Claudius, took this idea with a grain of salt. Others, for whatever reason, liked the idea. Domitian was one of them. He demanded that he be addressed as "Our Lord and God Domitian" by his subjects. This was a tough nut to chew for the Christian community, whose heart cry was that Jesus is Lord and there is no other.

In Paul's letters written between 45 and 63 A.D., Rome is viewed as an ally. Paul appeals to his Roman citizenship to avoid death threats by hostile Jewish groups. Paul even writes that the government is God's instrument to which the church should submit (Romans 13:1-7). But by 95 A.D., things had changed. The instrument of God had now become the enemy of God. It was the "Beast" to be resisted by all means, even unto death.

Traditionally, the John who wrote Revelation is identified as the John who walked with Jesus. He is also author of the Gospel that bears his name and of the three short epistles mentioned in the last chapter. In the opening chapter of Revelation we are told that John was a prisoner on the island of Patmos because of his faith in Jesus Christ (1:9).

Tradition tells us that after the destruction of Jerusalem in 70 A.D., John moved to Ephesus on the coast of Asia Minor. This was the same city where Paul spent several years during his third missionary journey. By 70 A.D., Paul was dead. John came to Ephesus and spent nearly thirty years as primary shepherd of the flock. He became known as "The Elder," a term of great honor.

When Domitian began to enforce emperor worship, he required every citizen in the empire to declare his or her allegiance publicly by burning a pinch of incense in honor of the emperor. To refuse was viewed as political treason. Some Christians capitulated to the pressure. Others, like John, took a stand.

One means to punish treason was banishment. If you were banished, your goods were confiscated and you were sent to a Roman penal colony such as Patmos, a rocky island near Ephesus where prisoners were forced to work in the mines. This was John's situation when he had the most amazing experience of his life. Exiled, banished, and subjected to harsh labor, John was visited by the risen Christ and given a vision. As instructed, John wrote what he saw.

Part One: The vision of Jesus

The book of Revelation can be divided into three main sections. The first is found in chapter 1 and contains the report of John's actual encounter with Jesus Christ. When Jesus appeared to John on Patmos, John was overwhelmed because he saw Jesus as he is. I think most of us tend to conceptualize Jesus as we see him in the Gospels. Certainly Christ's nature, his love and compassion, has not changed. But Jesus is no longer as he was in the Gospels in many important respects.

We know that in the act of incarnation, Jesus' glory was "veiled." Human corporeal flesh, which Jesus took on, could not fully express this glory. Remember that on the night before he went to the cross, Jesus spoke to the Father of once again manifesting the glory he shared with the Father from eternity past (John 17:5).

During Christ's earthly ministry, John was so intimate with Jesus that he sat next to him at dinner and as they reclined — the normal posture for eating — even laid his head on Jesus' chest. Now when John sees Jesus, he falls "at his feet as though dead" (1:17). Why? Because Jesus has a glorified body! It sounds religious, but it is much more. Were Jesus to walk in the room today, we would be overwhelmed and perhaps terrified His first words to us would likely be, "Don't be afraid." If you want to see Jesus as he is today, read Revelation 1.

John is unable to perfectly express this encounter because of the limitations of human language. He needs to rely on the poetic language of simile, finding similar concepts in daily reality to attempt to describe what Jesus is like. The word *like* found its way repeatedly into John's writing because so much of the vision is beyond common linguistic categories that he can only give rough equivalents.

This is the first "unveiling" of the book: Jesus Christ glorified, Lord of the church. Jesus stands in the midst of seven candlesticks. This imagery is symbolic and in this case we are even told the meaning of the symbol. The candlesticks represent the churches that make up the whole church. Jesus instructs John to write three things: (1) *that which you have seen*, (2) *that which is*, and (3) *that which will take place after these things* (1:19).

These instructions make a nice outline for the book. In chapter 1, John writes what he has seen: Jesus glorified. In chapters 2–3, John writes that which is: his seven letters to seven first-century churches describe the current spiritual condition of each. In chapters 4–22, he writes what will take place after these things — an apocalyptic odyssey into the future of human history and its final destiny.

PART TWO: LETTERS TO THE SEVEN CHURCHES

The theme of Revelation is quite simple: Jesus Christ is coming back! How this theme is communicated is at times quite complex. The easiest part of the book to understand is this one, in which Jesus dictates to John letters to seven churches in Asia Minor. These were the groups of Christ-followers that had originated from Paul's ministry out of Ephesus and over which John now had spiritual responsibility.

Each of these letters follows a first-century epistolary model and contains seven distinct and parallel features, beginning with a greeting and a description of the author. These introductory elements are followed by an analysis of the condition of the specific church to which the letter is addressed. The analysis comments on the good things going on in each church as well as problems that Jesus discerns in each. Where change is needed, the letter includes instruction or even rebuke. Where encouragement is needed, it is given. Finally, each letter ends with a promise of what Jesus will do if the church responds to his instruction.

Over the centuries, the book of Revelation and specifically the letters to the churches have been explored from a number of perspectives. The most obvious angle is to see the letters as primarily addressing seven actual churches in seven real cities at the time John wrote the book. The question becomes whether there is more here than the obvious.

Some have suggested that these seven churches represent the entire church of the first century. This theory is based on the significance that numbers played in apocalyptic literature. Seven, for example, was viewed as a number of wholeness or completeness. This view holds that in John's day there were many churches like the church in Ephesus that had lost their "first love," and the letter was intended to instruct such churches throughout the empire. A second hypothesis holds that somehow these seven churches represent seven types of churches that would appear repeatedly throughout history. Under this scenario Jesus picked these seven with their specific issues because as time went on, they would represent these reappearing models.

Another theory suggests that these seven churches represent seven periods of church history. This theory holds that these seven periods would unfold between the time of the vision and the return of Christ. Thus Ephesus represents the first- century church, followed by a "Smyrna period," a "Pergamum period," and so on.

In the last days preceding Christ's return, the church would be in the pathetic state of the Laodicean church, about which he had nothing good to say. Those who embrace this theory tend to have very different ideas of exactly how to break down the timeline and how to assign the messages to specific periods.

However we view these letters, they are valuable for all churches in every age because we know "all Scripture is God- breathed and is useful for teaching, rebuking, correcting and training in righteousness" (2 Timothy 3:16). A careful study of these chapters is extremely challenging both corporately and individually.

If you were to summarize the messages of the seven letters, it might look something like this:

Letter One: To Ephesus — Rekindle your love for Jesus. Letter Two: To Smyrna — Faithfully endure persecution. Letter Three: To Pergamum — Resist compromise.
Letter Four: To Thyatira — Avoid apostasy.
Letter Five: To Sardis — Recognize your condition. Letter Six: To Philadelphia — Keep up the good work. Letter Seven: To Laodicea — Get serious about your faith.

These messages set the stage for what follows in Revelation. In a sense, Jesus is saying, "If you are going to make it through the coming times, you need these seven spiritual qualities."

PART THREE: THINGS TO COME

Chapter 4 heralds the futuristic dimension of Revelation, beginning with a phrase in Greek that means "after these things." The logical reference is to the things spoken of in Revelation 2–3. For those who view the book as containing a message that transcends the first century, chapters 4–22 are yet to be fulfilled.

It is important to understand that just as interpreters have looked at the letters to the churches in various ways, so too for this section. Some scholars and teachers believe that the message of the future was only for first-century application. For instance, to a first-century audience the Beast would have been the Roman Empire persecuting the church at the time. If you understand the book from this perspective, it contains little future prediction.

Others believe these chapters have been fulfilled in the history of the church from the first century to our own day. They attempt to interpret Revelation's symbolic images by identifying them with events that have already occurred.

The predominant view throughout church history has been that these things are yet to occur. If you hold this understanding, then much of the book awaits the dawning of the final years of human history and the coming of what the Old Testament prophets called the Day of the Lord.

The interpretive key to these chapters revolves around a series of events that John sees take place in heaven, each of which has repercussions on earth. The heavenly events are organized around three sets of seven judgments God executes on the earth to bring his plans and purposes to fulfillment.

The first of these judgments involves a Lamb in heaven opening seven seals found on a scroll given to him by "him who sat on the throne." The opening of this scroll initiates all the events contained in the rest of the book. The symbolism of the scroll is relatively easy to understand. Scrolls often contained messages given by God to the prophets. This scroll contains God's final plans for our planet. As Jesus Christ opens each seal

—the Lamb who was slain and yet lives — cataclysmic events occur on earth.

The opening of the seventh seal introduces the reader to seven angels with seven trumpets. Each set of judgments intensifies over the previous set. The second set of judgments is usually called the trumpet judgments. As each angel sounds his trumpet in heaven, acts of judgment take place on the earth. The devastation is of such magnitude that we can hardly conceive what this period of time will be like.

A couple of major themes permeate this section of Revelation. Along with the theme of God's final judgment being executed on the planet, another involves "the saints." Depending upon your school of thought, these saints are understood as either the generation of Christian believers still living when these events occur or as the final generation of the people of Israel. In the latter view the saints are those Jews who come to faith in Jesus as Messiah after the believing church has been removed from earth by a pre-tribulation rapture (a theological position teaching that the church is "caught up" to be with Jesus prior to the beginning of the tribulation period).

During the execution of the judgments, the saints are protected from God's wrath but subjected to persecution by a hostile world. In a series of interludes between the seals, the trumpets, and the bowls, pictures of this conflict are portrayed in symbolic visions. Each vision is designed to give the same primary message: remain faithful through persecution and eventually you will be rewarded. This was an especially relevant message to the first-century audience of the book.

When the seventh angel sounds his trumpet, two events occur. The first is the appearance of seven final angels who hold golden bowls. The outpouring of the bowls' contents will complete the redemptive judgment of God. With the sounding of the trumpet, the scene in heaven is one of celebration as a proclamation is made that the kingdom of the world will once more be under the reign of God and his Son, Jesus Christ.

The bowl judgments lead to a complete devastation of the planet. That which was partial in the seals and trumpets reaches fulfillment with the outpouring of the bowls. The climax of this set of judgments is a gathering of all the world's armies at a place called Armageddon. A Hebrew word meaning "the mountain of Megiddo," it refers to a wide plain running through the middle of Israel where many of the nation's great battles were fought.

It is during the final phase of this battle, described in chapter 19, that Revelation reaches its central event. Jesus Christ returns to earth. He comes as the conquering king. He comes to reclaim what is rightfully his. He comes to establish once and for all time the kingdom of God on earth. He comes to put an end to all that has plagued humanity since the Fall. He comes to end the reign of evil.

Christ's return is followed by a series of events that bring the book to a close. The thousand-year reign of Christ on earth, known as the Millennium, is pictured in chapter 20. How you understand this chapter depends again on your theological frame of reference. Some scholars view this as a literal thousand-year reign following Jesus' return. Some see it as the age of the church being climaxed by the return of Christ, while still others interpret the event symbolically. Theological terms like premillennialism, postmillennialism, and amillennialism have all been coined around interpretations of this chapter.

Revelation's final two chapters picture the end of history, as we know it and the beginning of the age to come. Earth is changed in an instant and a new earth is created. John sees the New Jerusalem descending from heaven to be the central fixture of this new earth. This New Jerusalem is the manifestation of God and his people dwelling together. In the center of the city is the Tree of Life, the same tree found in the Garden of Eden in the book of Genesis. The story of this marvelous book we call the Bible has come full circle. That which was once denied because of humanity's rebellion is now made accessible through the power of God and the cross of Jesus Christ.

FINAL WORDS
The book of Revelation closes with an invitation. The risen and reigning Christ simply says, "Come." It is as if Jesus is saying, "All this is for you. All you have to do is decide to receive it." From beginning to end, the marvelous love of God and his plans for humanity are invitations to life. This is the ultimate message and purpose of Scripture.

ENJOYING THE BIBLE: LIVING THE WORD
Now that we have come to the end of our journey through the Bible, it seems fitting that the final strategy for enjoying the Bible should be the strategy of living the Word. In the last chapter I mentioned the final element required in effective communication of biblical truth — *ethos*. *Ethos* has to do with the character of the communicator or teacher and how the Bible has transformed it. Effective communication of biblical truth is a matter of *logos* (content) delivered with *pathos* (passion) through *ethos* (character that validates the *logos* and *pathos*).

The Bible is a book designed to change our lives. It was never intended to be purely informational. It is always designed to be transformational. If we are really going to enjoy the Bible, we need to integrate its truths. There are two great tragedies regarding the Bible in the modern world. One is the tragedy of those who know virtually nothing about this book.

Western civilization was built on the truth of the Bible and the application of its principles into social and political systems. The best of Western law, economics, art, morality, and spirituality had their foundations in the Bible. For centuries, the Bible was the basis for education. Most members of society had a working understanding of its stories and teachings. More copies of the Bible were produced and purchased than any other book in the history of printing. Yet today in most Western nations the Bible is becoming a forgotten book.

We live in a time of biblical illiteracy. Though many of America's institutions of higher education, including Harvard, Princeton, Yale, and Brown, originally were founded to train ministers in Bible knowledge and theology, today few colleges and universities offer courses in the Bible, even as literature. Even within the institutional church, it is estimated that most attendees have less than a sixth-grade understanding of the Bible.

But as tragic as the lack of biblical knowledge is, there is a greater tragedy. That is the tragedy of having the information contained in the Bible but not responding to it in such a way that changes our lives. In the words of James, it is possible to be "hearers" of the Word without being "doers" of it. To really be men of the Word, we need to learn to live the Word.

For more than forty years I have been involved in that part of the body of Christ known as the evangelical church. Evangelicals pride themselves on several important theological concepts, primary of which is the commitment to the Bible as the inspired Word of God. In short, Evangelicals believe the Bible. We tend to think we believe the Bible more than many other segments of the church. We pride ourselves on this. We are a people of the Book.

Now, let me share with you our main problem. Just yesterday I received a phone call from a friend who is the president of a Christian ministry in another city. He was calling to ask my advice on hiring a new staff person. I knew that this job candidate was a well-known leader in another Christian ministry and when I expressed my surprise, my friend told me that this person had left that ministry under terrible circumstances. In fact, the person had been so poorly treated that he was too embarrassed to tell me specifics.

There are two sides to every story and the details of this one are not important. What *is* important was my friend's observation after sharing the story. Because his ministry involves significant contact with virtually every sector of the church in America and around the world, his words hit home. He said that in his experience evangelicals tended to be the cruelest and most ruthless people he works with, especially those in leadership positions in Christian churches and ministries.

What is wrong with this picture? Somewhere, someone who knew the Word was not living the Word. If we hear but do not do, we are deceiving ourselves. As an evangelical I must confess that I am horribly guilty of this. I have several lifetimes' worth of information. My application and implementation of this information leave much to be desired.

The greatest way to enjoy the Bible is to put what it teaches into practice. A man of the Word obeys and applies that which God has taught him through the Scriptures. One of the classic texts in this regard is 2 Timothy 3:16-17 in which Paul reminds his not-so-young-any-longer protégé: "All Scripture is God-breathed ["inspired"] and is useful for teaching, rebuking, correcting and training in righteousness, so that the man of God may be thoroughly equipped for every good work."

Some of us are pretty good at affirming the first line of this text. In my neck of the theological woods we have gone to war over the issue of inspiration. Those who question the inspired nature of the Bible and its accuracy have historically become the enemy (and that enemy sadly includes those within the body of Christ).

Now don't get me wrong; I believe in the inspiration of the Bible. I also happen to believe it was without error in the original manuscripts (which no longer happen to exist!). I believe all it teaches is true. But that is not the primary thrust of this passage in 2 Timothy. The primary thrust of Paul's instruction was how the Bible was to be applied in the way we live. It is "useful," or "profitable" (NASB).

The great challenge of the church today is to live what the Bible teaches. It is supposed to be our manual not only for what we believe, but also for how we live. How can a group of men and women who hold tenaciously to the inspiration and inerrancy of the Bible turn around and be identified as cruel and ruthless? Again, something is wrong with this picture.

APPLICATION

Historically, we have talked about living the Bible as application. How can we apply what we have come to understand? Let me start with two straightforward suggestions:

1. When the Bible tells you that something you are doing is wrong, stop doing it.
2. When the Bible tells you to do something you are not currently doing, do it.

If you will commit yourself to following these two instructions, you will be light-years ahead of about 95 percent of the Christian world in living the Word. Let me illustrate.

Throughout the history of faith, men and women have understood that the Bible tells us we should give one-tenth of our income back to God (Malachi 3:10). (Actually, the New Testament suggests a tenth as just a starting point.) Usually that means we either give this money to our local church or a Christian ministry. How many Christians do you think obey this Scripture? Tragically, my hunch is not many. Ironically, the same pas- sage that instructs us to give the tithe promises that God will bless our socks off if we do. Other passages indicate that when we hold back that which is God's and spend it on ourselves, we create our own poverty (Haggai 1:6).

Let's look at another illustration. The Bible teaches that each of us has God-given gifts we are to use in serving others. How many Christians are actively exercising these gifts? Sadly, the percentage is not great.

I've been told that Mahatma Gandhi was a great admirer and student of Jesus. One day late in Gandhi's life, a Christian friend asked him why he had never become a Christian. Gandhi replied that he had never met a Christian who acted like Christ. What an indictment! I often wonder what might have happened had Gandhi lived to meet Mother Teresa?

At a very basic level, applying the Bible is taking anything you are learning in your reading, studying, listening, memorizing, meditating, or teaching, and doing what the text advocates. Look for one action or attitude you can adopt each day and put it into action. Become a doer of the Word.

FOLLOWING JESUS

There is another way of living the Word that is not quite as easy. It could be argued that the call of Christ on our lives is to "Follow me" (Matthew 4:19) instead of just "Believe in me." In fairness, it is very difficult to follow Jesus if you do not believe in him. I am personally convinced that we are expected to do both.

What does it mean to follow Jesus? In the context of the New Testament it was called discipleship. The original twelve were disciples or *mathetes*. The Greek word means "a learner" or "student or follower" and was used in the context of rabbis and disciples or teachers and students. Historically, a disciple was one who attached himself to an admired teacher to learn everything the teacher could teach him both verbally and by example. The disciple was not only an academic student, but also a life student. The student's goal was to master the knowledge of the teacher and to imitate his life. When Jesus invited the disciples to follow him, it was an invitation to enter into this kind of relationship.

Jesus certainly instructed the disciples. He delivered a great deal of content, much of it contained in the four gospels. But he did more than verbally instruct them. He modeled for them. The most obvious example was when he washed their feet in the Upper Room the night before he was crucified (John 13:1-17).

As the meal was being prepared, Jesus took off his coat, wrapped a towel around his waist, and began the job that belonged to the lowest-rank household slave. If you were too poor to own a slave, you washed your own feet. If you were poor and your buddies were poor, you certainly didn't wash each other's feet! This would have been considered below even a poor man's station in life.

It is hard to imagine what was going through the minds of these twelve men as their leader kneeled to wash their feet. Only Peter spoke what possibly was on everyone's mind. "No way!" would be a pretty accurate paraphrase (John 13:6). Jesus demanded that Peter allow him. Then he explained: "You call me 'Teacher' and 'Lord,' and rightly so, for that is what I am. Now that I, your Lord and Teacher, have washed your feet, you also should wash one another's feet. I have set you an example that you should do as I have done for you" (John 13:13-15).

Of course, this event was not really about feet, though in its historical context it was precisely about feet. The point is that if you are going to follow Jesus, you need to take the role of servant, even when it seems to be the worst job available. Taking the lowest place and doing the most unglamorous job is what a follower of Jesus does. How do you think we are all doing on this one?

To follow Jesus requires that we are so familiar with him that we know what to do in each and every situation — and then we do it. I honestly do not currently know one person on the planet who operates like this. It certainly is not what I see in many churches. Many churches in the western world today are run like corporations with as much jockeying for power and recognition as in any secular industry. Perhaps that is why we are so ineffective in impacting our culture.

In His Steps is a remarkable book written in 1896 by a Protestant minister from Wichita, Kansas, named Charles Sheldon. The book has sold over fifteen million copies in the last century. It is the story of a group of men and women who decide for one year to approach every decision and action by asking the question, "What would Jesus do?" In the book, the experiment was revolutionary. Not only were the people transformed, their church was transformed, and the entire city was transformed. It is a must-read.

Unfortunately, *In His Steps* is fictional. Fortunately, some people over the years have read the book and attempted to put it into practice. Unfortunately, most give up because it is too hard. Fortunately, some don't. Unfortunately, in recent times we have taken the book and its message and turned it into a business.

WWJD? What would Jesus do? I think a better way of putting it is WWJHMD? What would Jesus have *me* do? We can't be Jesus, but we can follow what he tells us to do. This requires depth and empowerment in our spiritual lives. This is the step of application.

You might be a man or woman who knows the Word. You might be a man or woman who believes the Word. You might even be a man or woman who teaches the Word. But until you begin to seek to *live* the Word, you will not truly enjoy the Word, and you will certainly not be a man or woman *of* the Word.

The End of the Adventure

In these past hundred and some pages I have attempted to accomplish two objectives. First, I have tried to help you understand the "big picture" of the greatest book in the world. Together we have taken a brief journey from the ages of Adam and Abraham all the way through the time of Jesus and into the days yet to come.

My hope is that when you think of the Bible now you are immediately able to break the "big book" down into seven logical divisions. When you think of the Old Testament you will remember that it is made up of history, poetry, and prophecy. When the New Testament is your area of focus, you will remember that logically it breaks down into the Gospels, the book of Acts, the letters, and Revelation.

What's more, I trust that when you think of these primary divisions you will have some sense of the content of each. You will know that the first five books contain the Law, or Torah, of the ancient people of Israel. You will remember that in the time of Abraham and his early descendants, when the patriarchal clan numbered only seventy, the people of the promise lived in Canaan and later moved down to Egypt. From Egypt God led them back to the land, and the seventy became millions.

You will be able to place any book of history in the context of whether it was pre-kingdom, United Kingdom, Divided Kingdom, exile, or restoration. You will know the difference between the Northern kingdom of Israel and the Southern kingdom of Judah.

When you move into the five books of poetry you will be able to place each within its historical context. You will remember that the Psalms are songs. Some are songs of joy and praise. Some are the blues tunes of tough times. Some are hard songs wishing vengeance on Israel's enemies.

When you read Job, you will see it as a Jewish screenplay acted out on some ancient stage or in the minds of its first readers. When you read Proverbs, you will know that you are reading the distilled wisdom of this ancient people. Ecclesiastes will remind you of the things that are really important in life. Song of Solomon will help you appreciate your wife and also remind you that your relationship with God is one of the lover and the beloved.

The prophets will no longer be a mystery to you. As you read each of these seventeen books, you will be able to place the message in the proper context of the history of Israel. You will know the difference between the Major Prophets and the Minor Prophets. You will remember that in the same way the first five historical books play a special role in Israel's history, the five Major Prophets hold a special place among the prophetic messages.

You will know that some of the prophets spoke to the Northern kingdom of Israel and that their messages went unheeded. You will remember that in 722 B.C. the Assyrians annihilated these ten tribes. You will know that some of the prophets spoke to the Southern kingdom of Judah and that a few were heard. Ultimately, you will remember that some of the prophets spoke of the Southern kingdom's conquest by the Babylonians and of the destruction of Jerusalem and the temple.

You will remember that a few of the prophets, such as Daniel and Ezekiel, were prophets of the exile and that they foretold the nation's return to the land and the rebuilding of Jerusalem. You will also remember that the final three prophets prophesied after the return and restoration, in anticipation of the coming Messiah.

Your understanding of the Old Testament at this point is greater than you could have ever imagined. Along with understanding the Old Testament, you have also been enjoying the Bible. You have learned a few new strategies for listening more effectively when you are in church or at a Bible study. You also know a bit more of what the teacher or preacher is saying because of your new mastery of the content and context of the various parts of God's Word. You are reading the Bible on a consistent basis. You have even started to study it.

When you read the New Testament, you now know how the four gospels fit together. You understand how the picture painted by the combination of the four provides a much better understanding of the life and teaching of Jesus. You have some sense that when you read a passage or hear a message from one of the Gospels, you can put it in the context of the various phases of Jesus' ministry and the various places he ministered.

You know that when you read Mark, you might actually be reading the Q source. At least you know it was the first of the four gospels to be written. When you encounter material in Matthew or Luke that seems familiar, you know that the first three gospels "see" things in the same way and share a great deal in common. You might actually remember the word *synoptic* and know what it means. You will appreciate the Gospel of John even more because you know it was written much later than the other three and contains many great events in the life of Jesus not included in the other accounts.

When you read or study Acts you will know you are encountering the early church in action. You will remember that the early chapters of Acts focus on the church's Jewish dimension with Peter as its leader. When you move into the second half of the book you will know that Paul is the focus, and you will be able to track his movements. You will know how Paul's missionary journeys are related to the letters that follow in the next section of the New Testament.

You will be able to distinguish between the Pauline Epistles and the General Epistles. You now know that each of these documents was written to address specific situations occurring in actual groups of believers in the first century. Your ability to integrate the letter with the book of Acts or your knowledge of early church history will make these letters come alive.

As you were learning about these letters, you were also developing tools to better enjoy the Bible. You have become a student. You are heeding the exhortation to "study to show yourself approved." You have learned helpful tools to make your study more profitable. When you read certain books, you will be building outlines of the major themes and how the author develops these themes.

You also will be building a library of tools to make your Bible study even more enjoyable and profitable. You will take time to make sure you understand what a passage or a word really means or to clarify ancient cultural items and issues.

Your enjoyment of the Bible is growing rapidly as you memorize certain passages. Your life is benefiting from your time in God's Word as you mediate on the meaning and significance of the things you are reading. You are building an internal spiritual resource base as God's Word becomes more and more integrated into your life.

Finally, you have a good understanding of what the future holds. You are one of the minority of Christians who has some sense of what John was attempting to communicate in the book of Revelation. You know that the vision John received tells you much about what Jesus is really like. You have studied the seven letters and know what Jesus said to those seven churches and how these messages have relevance for today.

You have seen the future. You know that one day the king-doms of man will fall and the kingdom of God will triumph. You know that the very same Jesus you have come to know through the Gospels is coming again. You have submitted your life to him and know that when he comes, you will be with him forever.

All your understanding of the Bible and your enjoyment of learning how to master it have created a desire to integrate its truth into your own life. You have begun to see how understand-ing leads to application, which yields the maximum measure of enjoyment. If these things are true of you, then my time writing this book has been well spent.

About the Author

§

BOB BELTZ IS THE SENIOR Pastor of Highline Community Church in Greenwood Village, Colorado, and President of The Telos Project, a non-profit corporation based in Littleton, Colorado, seeking to influence contemporary, post-modern culture with faith and family-friendly projects.

Over the last sixteen years Bob has been a special advisor to the Anschutz Corporation, the parent company of Walden Media. In this role Bob helped in the development, production, and marketing of such films as *Joshua, The Lion, the Witch and the Wardrobe, Amazing Grace: the William Wilberforce Story, Prince Caspian, and The Voyage of the Dawn Treader*. Bob served as a producer on Mark Burnett and Roma Downey's Emmy nominated *The Bible* series, the movie *Son of God*, and the NBC series *A.D.: the Bible Continues*.

Bob is the author of fifteen books including the novels *Somewhere Fast, Lilith Redeemed,* and *She Loves You,* the best-selling *Daily Disciplines for the Christian Man,* and an update of William Wilberforce's *Real Christianity,* published in conjunction with the film *Amazing Grace*. He writes a blog at bobbeltz.com, and co-hosts the weekly radio program "You Get the Blessing".

Bob is a graduate of the University of Missouri, and Denver Seminary where he earned both his Master of Arts and Doctor of Ministry degrees. Bob's wife of over forty years, Allison, is a religious liberty and human rights advocate. He has a married daughter, Stephanie, a son, Baker, and three grandchildren, Olivia, Emma, and Jaxon. When not writing, teaching, or making movies, Bob can usually be seen heading into the mountains of Colorado on his Harley-Davidson with a group of cultural infidels.